W9-ANK-560

Euclid Public Library
631 E. 222nd Street
Euclid, Ohio 44123
216-261-5300

AMERICAN FREEMASONRY

Its Revolutionary History *and* Challenging Future

ALAIN DE KEGHEL, 33°

TRANSLATED BY JON E. GRAHAM

Inner Traditions
Rochester, Vermont • Toronto, Canada

Inner Traditions
One Park Street
Rochester, Vermont 05767
www.InnerTraditions.com

Copyright © 2015 by Éditions Dervy
English translation copyright © 2017 by Inner Traditions International

Originally published in French under the title *Le Défi Maçonnique Américain* by
    Éditions Dervy
First U.S. edition published in 2017 by Inner Traditions

All rights reserved. No part of this book may be reproduced or utilized in
any form or by any means, electronic or mechanical, including photocopying,
recording, or by any information storage and retrieval system, without permission
in writing from the publisher.

Library of Congress Cataloging-in-Publication Data
Names: Keghel, Alain de, author.
Title: American freemasonry : its revolutionary history and challenging
    future / Alain de Keghel, 33° ; translated by Jon E. Graham.
Other titles: Le Défi Maçonnique Américain. English
Description: First U.S. edition. | Rochester, Vermont : Inner Traditions,
    2017. | "Originally published in French under the title Le Défi Maçonnique
Américain by Éditions Dervy." | Includes bibliographical references and index.
Identifiers: LCCN 2017020633 (print) | LCCN 2017005915 (e-book) |
    ISBN 9781620556054 (hardcover) | ISBN 9781620556061 (e-book)
Subjects: LCSH: Freemasonry—United States—History.
Classification: LCC HS515 (print) | LCC HS515 .K4413 2017 (e-book) |
    DDC 366/.10973—dc23
LC record available at https://lccn.loc.gov/2017005915

Printed and bound in Canada by Friesens Corporation

10   9   8   7   6   5   4   3   2   1

Text design and layout by Priscilla Baker
This book was typeset in Garamond Prmier Pro with Bembo, Shelley Script, and
Helvetica Neue used as display typefaces

To send correspondence to the author of this book, mail a first-class letter to the
author c/o Inner Traditions • Bear & Company, One Park Street, Rochester, VT
05767, and we will forward the communication, or contact the author directly at
keghel.s@gmail.com.

Contents

Appendices

Foreword

By Margaret C. Jacob, Ph.D.

Perhaps it takes a Frenchman to explain American Freemasonry. Certainly Alain de Keghel knows the subject well, both its history and its contemporary situation. It helps that he has lived in the United States and has studied its general history. This book accepts the challenges posed by American Freemasonry, by its piety about God and country and its refusal to entertain foreign influences. The British origins are clearly important, and the association of the lodges with the American Revolution gives a respectability that few other forms of civil society can claim.

Yet even that association could not save the lodges from a virulent anti-Masonry faction that emerged in the 1820s as a result of the Morgan Affair. The account de Keghel gives of it is balanced and fair and rightly links the notion of there having been a Masonic conspiracy to a mind-set that reappeared after 1945 and is generally labeled as "McCarthyism," named after the vociferous, Communist-hunting U.S. senator Joseph McCarthy.

This book is also about Freemasonry in Canada and contains a very helpful section on French American Masonic relations, which have often been tumultuous. Members on either side of the Atlantic will recognize many elements in these ruptures, among them the issue of God's existence and the presence of many women in the French lodges. Perhaps hardest of all to understand is the split in American Freemasonry between lodges for blacks and those for whites. Anyone who has ever addressed lodges in the American South will have witnessed that sad reality. One of the earliest members of a Paris lodge is described in the letters as "a Negro trumpeter in the King's Guard." French Freemasonry has a great deal to be proud about in its history. As Freemasonry has reached the three-hundredth anniversary of the founding of the Grand Lodge of London in 1717, the American lodges have found a charitable and wise interpreter.

MARGARET C. JACOB, PH.D.

MARGARET C. JACOB, PH.D., is a professor of history at the University of California, Los Angeles. One of the world's foremost Masonic scholars, she is considered a pioneer in the field of the history of civil society, with emphasis on Masonic history. Her work in the early development of Freemasonry documents connections between early European Freemasons and the Craft as we know it today. She is the author of *The Radical Enlightenment: Pantheists, Freemasons, and Republicans; Living the Enlightenment: Freemasonry and Politics in Eighteenth-Century Europe;* and *The Origins of Freemasonry: Facts and Fictions.*

Foreword

❧

By Arturo de Hoyos, 33°

The history of Freemasonry in general and American Freemasonry in particular receives less attention than the practice of the rites, on which authors more often focus their studies. This should be seen as most likely responding to the primary interests of their readers. They are seeking first and foremost access to knowledge about the Masonic initiatory path. The rarest works are those seeking to shed light on and decipher the developments of the Masonic order from its beginnings, with an eye to their interaction with contemporary challenges. Both of these approaches are of equal importance to the grand archivist and grand historian of the Southern Jurisdiction. The articles published in the magazine *Heredom* attest to this reality.

Relatively few in number in comparison to the members of the lodges are those Freemasons who belong to the research societies, but far rarer are the French Freemasons who have been consistently involved over a long period of years with studies of this nature in the United States. The authentic knowledge that can be found in the depths of the archives is capable of providing a solid foundation for positions. The library of the Southern Jurisdiction of the Ancient and Accepted Scottish Rite, housed in the House of the Temple in Washington, D.C., figures at the very forefront of the world's collections of Masonic documents. It contains a wealth of information and documentation that begs to be used. It was at this already mythic site that the noted Masonic writer Albert Pike labored at the end of the nineteenth century. He has left us an invaluable legacy on which researchers are still tirelessly working. But there is also the legacy of Albert Mackey and many other major figures of our Masonic history.

Alain de Keghel has been a lifetime member of the Scottish Rite Research Society of the Southern Jurisdiction since the 1990s. He did not content himself with the title alone but instead used this membership to cultivate sustained, friendly, fraternal, and studious relations with the large family of American researchers. People will remember that it was he who, in 1999, carried out research with Pierre Mollier, the director of the Library and Archives of the Grand Orient of France, and myself on behalf of the French Masonic magazine *Renaissance traditionnelle* by consulting documents of the highest importance at the site of our library of the Southern Jurisdiction. The results were seen in the April 2000 issue, no. 122, of this magazine. The article focused on the beginnings of the Ancient and Accepted Scottish Rite in France. It was structured around the discovery of an exceptional document: the first book of the architecture of the original French Supreme Council, from 1804 to 1812.

Nor was it any accident that Alain de Keghel took part in the commemoration festivities of the bicentennial of the Ancient and Accepted Scottish Rite in Charleston, South Carolina, in September 2001, as his involvement far surpassed any particularisms. We are familiar with his Masonic eclecticism, his participation in the American society of the Philalethes, as well as in that of the research lodge Quatuor Coronati no. 8 (Bayreuth, Germany), and in the famous first International Conference on the History of Freemasonry, held in Edinburgh in 2007. These conferences have been highly successful, and one was even held in Alexandria, Virginia. The 2015 conference was held at the Bibliothèque Nationale in Paris.

This openness to the diversity of our Order is also the fruit of Alain de Keghel's long experience as a Mason, which has been quite varied, geographically speaking, and even includes Japan, where the author served as a career diplomat. In addition to fifty years steeped in the ideals of the pastor James Anderson's tradition, he has acquired an exceptional range of knowledge, which he is sharing with us today. It is most definitely the case here for the United States, where, during the time he was posted here as a diplomat, he forged fraternal relationships to which he remains ever faithful.

This book devoted here to the challenge of American Freemasonry will assuredly hold the attention of both American and French readers. It retraces the lines that are essential for a good understanding of the American Masonic era. The precocious and close ties between French and American Freemasons are put into perspective and offer us a golden opportunity to recall the wealth of our shared legacy, particularly the Ancient and Accepted Scottish Rite, which is naturally Franco-American, strictly speaking. Avoiding all clichés, the author offers a path that permits us to move closer to the actual realities. He even goes so far as to indulge—perhaps this is a professional quirk—in a speculative and prospective study that offers evidence of a protracted observation of the American Masonic and sociopolitical stage.

The reader will also note the author's stab at an outline for the future of new and exogenous French experiences in North America. Although this aspect remains a marginal one in comparison with the essential examination of the American Masonic entity, it is not lacking in interest. In fact, it offers evidence of the enduring nature of the effort put forth by French and American Freemasons in the quest of a shared fraternity, although we are also all well aware of its limits. History teaches how these paths are sowed with pitfalls. Indeed, here is where we find the weight of history, that of cultural differences as well as those of religion and tradition. The major figures that he invokes will stick in the mind, however: the Marquis de Lafayette and his close friends George Washington and Benjamin Franklin. Franklin was the elder of the Lodge of the Nine Sisters (*les Neufs Soeurs*) in Paris and a friend of Voltaire. But we also have Alexandre François Auguste de Grasse-Tilly, who played a major role in the spread of the Ancient and Accepted Scottish Rite through Europe upon his return from America.

However, we all know that institutional Masonic relations obey rules that do not always encourage relationships. France, the sole European power to have never been engaged in armed conflict against the United States, is also the power that came to the aid of the American revolutionaries, albeit not always as a forgiving partner. France does figure, however, among the ranks of loyal allies, and, during this current period of centennial commemoration of the First World War, this Franco-American fraternity has been warmly celebrated in Normandy. Alexis de Tocqueville was among the first to take it upon himself to explain America to France. This is exactly what Alain de Keghel is doing today to make the reality of American Freemasonry better known.

In our now globalized world, the stakes are necessarily different from those in play at the birth of the Masonic order, which will soon celebrate its three-hundredth birthday. By giving his book the title *American Freemasonry: Its Revolutionary History and Challenging Future,* Alain de Keghel has chosen an approach that draws from the wellsprings of our history, which he marches forth with the intention of projecting it into the future, where new stakes will be in play. His cautious but insightful judgments are not without value for an American researcher, who will most likely see it as a mirror carried by an initiate offering this reflection.

ARTURO DE HOYOS, 33°

ARTURO DE HOYOS is the grand archivist and grand historian (director of the museum and library) of the Southern Jurisdiction of the Ancient and Accepted Scottish Rite in the United States.

Interpreting American Freemasonry throughout Time

It is certainly no accident that my choice of a title for this book contains a reference to Jean-Jacques Servan-Schreiber's renowned *American Challenge*. This was not only because our paths crossed at the beginning of the 1990s and Jean-Jacques Servan-Schreiber then wished to show a sign of his esteem to me. No, what fundamentally inspired this choice was the vision of someone who during the WWII postwar period devoted himself to a complete examination of what he had observed of the United States in order to put the pieces of a very complex puzzle together and shout, "There is still time to take action!"

His motivation was certainly not philosophical in nature. He sought to sensitize Europe and France to the huge stakes raised by the ever-louder assertion of what Hubert Védrine would later call "the American hyperpower." On this subject, Andreas Önnerfors writes, "We are not facing a classic political imperialism, a will to conquer, but the more mechanical presence of an overflow of power due to the difference of the 'pressure' between North America and the rest of the world, Europe included. This high-powered nature of America is felt but poorly understood. It has been the subject almost everywhere of significant documentation. But as its most novel character is acceleration, what is known becomes quickly outdated."[1]

My concerns and observations are restricted here to the Masonic order in its American, global, and geopolitical dimension. But this book naturally has the ambition to call for a realization of what is happening and for preparations to be made; French and European Freemasons cannot allow themselves to remain indifferent spectators. This too is the assembling of a puzzle that is more complex than it may appear.

The fact is that the Freemasonry of North America is different in many respects from that of the continental grand lodges. It is equally dissimilar to the obediences of Great Britain. This domain is fairly misunderstood by those outside of North America, after all, with the exception of a certain number of French Freemasons who spend time there as members of the sole grand lodge in France, the Grande Loge Nationale Française (GLNF), which enjoys regular recognition from its counterpart on the other side of the Atlantic. This organization lost its privilege of international recognition quite recently, following a split and the crises it experienced in 2013 after its grand master was dismissed because of his questioned management.

Here we will have the opportunity to devote ourselves to the developments that are essential for grasping the criteria of regularity and "recognition," as stated and defined by the United Grand Lodge of England—and consequently applied within the boundaries of the American grand lodges. The fact remains, however, that because of such doctrinaire arrangements, the brothers of the GLNF are practically the sole group to have access to American Masonic temples. Others, who live in the United States, have also sometimes had the opportunity to discover this extremely rare Masonic world that gives chance human encounters full opportunity to flourish. But this is only one of the many aspects of American Freemasonry, which possesses many facets that are equally unknown. It is therefore important to dissect them in order to present them to individuals outside this world, while not overlooking the evolutions of a Masonic entity that experienced the undulations of a society known for its plasticity.

It is through a deliberately open approach, which has been cleared of clichés to the greatest extent possible, that I have chosen to tackle these numerous aspects of a subject that is so little understood and sometimes described in very broad lines with little attention to subtleties. It is fairly common knowledge that in the United States, as elsewhere, Masonry is founded on a tradition that will soon be three hundred years old. The grand lodges govern a certain number of arrangements that apply to their jurisdictional boundaries and therefore to the lodges of the symbolic grades. The high councils of the Ancient and Accepted Scottish Rite do as much for the lodges of the high grades. These two spheres, which complement each other, exhibit unique features that distinguish one from the other.

But the Anglo-Saxon connections hardly exclude the special features of the Americans, and this gives us a field of observation to study while unwinding the storyline like a documentary. The American Masonic order is complex and sometimes difficult to define for those who grew up in a European social and cultural environment and who have only lightly brushed the actual realities during far too brief journeys to these distant shores.

We shall additionally see that American Freemasons also claim, rightfully, traditional roots that they share with their "separated brothers" of the Old World. French Freemasonry, like that of London, looks like a strand of Ariadne's thread here. So there should not be any problem accepting the composite historical line of descent that connects them while wisely keeping a distance from the doctrine. However, one essential factor will be that of their sensibilities concerning identity and their reference points, which have become quite different over the course of what will soon be three centuries of existence for the Order.

A study of American Freemasonry will therefore not entirely escape from an approach that partially falls into the categories of sociology and ethnology. The acceleration of history in a world marked by the shifting of demographic, economic, and political centers of gravity and diplomatic priorities also makes it essential that we take into account the major tendencies of the evolution of American society.

The decline of American Freemasonry, while real to a certain extent, also deserves an analysis to assess the true scope of this decline without falling into the pathos of its decadence or panegyrics concerning its renaissance. The shape taken by the impact of American developments on the Order as a whole is also one of the questions that necessarily arise. But this line of questioning remains pertinent, whether what is being examined is its influence in American civil society or its weight on the profane international stage.

Lastly, this study—which is too succinct to lay claim to being exhaustive—*would* have contained a significant gap if I had not attempted an evaluation of the impact that the establishment of liberal obediences and jurisdictions (with the lodges of the Grand Orient de France [GODF; Grand Orient of France] in the forefront) in the United States did or could have; some of these obediences and jurisdictions include black and/or female members. All share the commonality of not belonging to the institutional American Masonic system, strictly speaking, and living on its margins—which does not, however, forbid contacts of a limited nature, limits that are quickly reached.

It is therefore necessary to include here an overview of the establishment of exogenous Masonic entities in America while also braving an essential incursion into neighboring Quebec, as the bonds of proximity between the two countries are so strong. On the other hand, falling within the jurisdiction of another tropism, Freemasonry in Mexico is not discussed here despite its inclusion, along with that of the United States and Canada, in the nebula of the permanent Conference of the Grand Lodges of North America.

This book, which is essentially based on information gathered during recent studies, has no other objective than to offer the reader a general overview accompanied by suggestions for future study. This should entice the more curious to expand their knowledge by consulting the many texts and documents listed in the bibliography. This includes old documents that are taken as authoritative and, more importantly, more recent texts. It offers reading and consultation suggestions by going to the most pertinent sources.

This book lastly includes a color insert that eloquently illustrates the course taken by the Masonic order in the United States as well as the Franco-American historical connections symbolized by emblematic figures such as Benjamin Franklin, Marie-Joseph Paul Yves Roch Gilbert du Motier, the marquis de Lafayette, and Alexandre François Auguste de Grasse-Tilly.

I would like to thank the many American Freemasons who opened their archives to me and provided me with the documents that are essential to accurately grasp the evolution of the Order and its various components in the United States.

I would like to particularly thank the grand archivist and grand historian of the Supreme Council of the Southern Jurisdiction at the House of the Temple in Washington, D.C., Arturo de Hoyos, who wrote one of the forewords for this book. He clearly sought to facilitate my consultations on-site with no other consideration than that of historical research and a feeling of fraternity that was never found wanting.

May S. Brent Morris, former editor of the excellent publication *Heredom,* also find here an expression of my gratitude; Morris, like myself, is also a lifetime member of the Scottish Rite Research Society.

I finally come to my longtime friend John L. Cooper III, grand master of the Grand Lodge of California and current president of the Conference of the Grand Masters of North America, who took upon himself the responsibility to write the afterword of this book. How could I ever forget the fortunate joint initiative that allowed us to organize a seminar together in 2003, in Sacramento, California, when he was secretary general of his obedience, a seminar during which the grand master of the GODF, Alain Bauer, was invited to speak—an extremely rare event.

Bauer caused a sensation, notably during his famous exchanges with Tom Jackson, then president of the Commission on Information for Recognition of the Conference of Grand Masters. Bauer engaged with Jackson in humorous, retrospective hypothetical speculations on the famous rules of recognition, which take up considerable space in the Grand Orient. Some might say "this was no big deal," but it was definitely one of the most charming pages of our recent history of external relations.

This was another exceptional moment of a too-rare and fruitful complicity between a grand commander and grand master: not competing but engaged together in a confident and completely uninhibited approach with an eye toward what is best for the standing of the obedience and its values. And this inside a zone that had remained unexplored, sealed off, and dreaded until then as an unknown. Here reference does not require reverence. Therefore it was a realpolitik, essentially constructed on an international network of the Ancient and Accepted Scottish Rite, which has already been labeled by some as the "new doctrine of joint external policy."

The GODF continues to draw dividends from this, but upon closer examination it can be seen that this benefit is also shared by our California brethren. This groundbreaking exercise of dialogue was repeated in Los Angeles in 2005 and again in San Francisco in 2009. By accepting the task of writing the afterword, John L. Cooper III has clearly confirmed that his exceptional spirit of fraternal openness knows no bounds. I would like to thank him most particularly.

I would also like to extend my gratitude to René Le Moal, director of the collection of Éditions Dervy—in which this book first appeared—and a tireless adviser, gratitude equaled only by his unbroken granite-like support, which had been previously demonstrated by the publication of an earlier essay for Éditions Vega in 2009.

My ultimate sign of gratitude is reserved for Erika Peschard-Erlih, the ever-attentive reader who aided me in avoiding the reefs with which all authors are familiar.

Finally, a tiny wink to history: it was on the shores of Lake Leman, at Coppet Castle, made famous by Madame de Staël (née Anne Louise Germaine Necker), that the final touches were put on this book, which looks at the facets of a world that is no longer only dominated by America but also characterized more by the growing interdependence of all societies. Freemasonry cannot escape this evolution either.

PARIS, JUNE 2014
ALAIN DE KEGHEL

Freemasonry in Pioneer America

The First Lodges and Their Context

To consider the advent of the Masonic order and its genesis at the very beginning of the history of the United States—from the first half of the eighteenth century—is to plunge into the complex maze of a new space containing notions that are hard for twenty-first-century Europeans and Americans to grasp. This current century is dominated by the fruits of a rich intellectual and philosophical proliferation that has developed since that time. The French and American Revolutions passed through this way, but so did many philosophers and thinkers whose works remained theoretical.

So it is quite important to be firmly situated in the historical perspective of thought and also to transpose into it the religious and philosophical perspectives of the initial century of the Enlightenment in the Old World and not lose sight of the restrictions that prevailed in many lands (where religious practice was not truly free if it was considered to be a deviation from the dominant religion—that of the sovereign). It was often freedom to practice their faith, not the search for material well-being, that motivated the first emigrants who settled in New England.

For an accurate understanding and appreciation of the context, it is therefore crucial to revisit the history of ideas. Bernard Le Bouvier de Fontenelle writes, "We are illuminated by the lights of the true religion and, in my belief, by several rays of the true philosophy."[1]

In a commentary on this subject, Jacques Roger notes that "this is how very different values of the same image stood out at the beginning of the sixteenth century. In the singular, light [*lumière*] was an emanation of the absolute; in the plural, the Enlightenment's discoveries [*Lumières*] are primarily the slow acquisitions of humanity over the course of its history."[2]

It is essential for a good reading of what occurred in America at its beginnings as well as what has persisted in American mind-sets, to be fully aware of this.

Freedom of conscience and the free exercise of beliefs and religions are two consubstantial references for the immigration that founded America. It is, moreover, the first amendment of the Constitution of the United States that provides the most perfect example of this. Ratified in 1791, in a corpus of ten amendments known as the Bill of Rights, it forbids the United States Congress from adopting any laws that restrict the freedom of religion and expression, freedom of the press, and the right to peaceably assemble. While this amendment only refers to the federal government, it is legally accepted that it also applies to the state legislatures of the union. Its principles also come equally into play in the decisions made by the executive and judiciary branches.

As an expansion on the previous observations, it could also be helpful to recall here all the symbolism connected to the famous ship the *Mayflower,* which made land on the East Coast of America on November 26, 1620. It had weighed anchor on September 6 in Plymouth, England, to sail to America with one hundred or so passengers onboard (about whom it is a good idea to recall that some thirty-six of them were very pious English Protestants who had been expelled from England by King James I). Poorly prepared to settle in an inhospitable environment and arriving when autumn was almost over, they could not devote themselves to the agrarian labor essential for their survival, and half of them succumbed to disease. It was thanks to the help of the Patuxet Indians that the survivors learned how to grow corn as well as how to hunt and fish, the activities that allowed them to establish the first bases of colonization. In thanks to God and the Patuxet Indians, the colonialists decided to have a feast together at the time that the Indians already celebrated the end of the harvest; this new holiday they christened Thanksgiving. It was an act of spontaneous syncretism by the Protestant Pilgrims; President Lincoln would declare this tradition a national holiday in 1863.

It would be more than one hundred years after the arrival of the *Mayflower* on American soil before traces of actually structured and documented Masonic activity would appear. As many authors before me have observed, even in England, Freemasonry was at this time still in its archaic, primitive state.

A certain number of lodges, often quite far from one another, were then active in the New World. They soon saw the necessity of attaining obediential cohesion by placing themselves under the authority of a provincial grand master. This grand master would, ideally, be named by the grand master of the Grand Lodge of England, with jurisdiction over the states of New York, New Jersey, and Pennsylvania. The responsibilities of this position would fall to a soldier, Colonel Daniel Coxe.

The first supporting documents date only from July 30, 1733. These are the annals of the Grand Lodge Saint John of the Orient, in Philadelphia, recording the appointment of Henry Price by the Duke of Montagu, grand master of England, to the duties of the provincial grand master of North America. Merely one year later, Benjamin Franklin published the first American version of Pastor James Anderson's *The Constitutions of the Free-Masons,* which was also the first Masonic work to be published in the American colonies (see plate 1 for an image of its title page). Shortly thereafter, Franklin would be given the responsibilities of provincial grand master for Pennsylvania.

During the months immediately following his appointment,

Franklin shared with the grand master of London the wishes of the Freemasons of his jurisdiction to elect a provincial grand master and his advisers, in the expectation that an autonomous grand master would be established for America. This move was very likely ahead of its time, but it heralded the affirmation of the American brothers' desire for emancipation that was already making itself heard in Europe. Yet it would not be until 1778, two years after the Declaration of Independence was signed on July 4, 1776, in Philadelphia, that the official separation with the Grand Lodge of England would take place.

In fact, obediential territorial authority was no longer exercised in Boston by the Grand Lodge of England alone, which therefore found itself in a position of "concurrence." Another lodge, the Lodge of Saint Andrew, which derived its authority from the Grand Lodge of Scotland, was established in 1752. It asserted its autonomy by authoritatively adopting the title of Independent Grand Lodge of Massachusetts. The loyalist Grand Lodge Saint John saw a gradual decline starting from this time that eventually induced it to bow to reality and accept a merger with the Grand Lodge of Massachusetts.

Crisscrossed by opposing currents—loyalists against the patriotic supporters of the American Revolution—and heir as well to the famous quarrels concerning rites between Ancients and Moderns, this first American obedience, strictly speaking, experienced the vicissitudes of the troubled times through which society as a whole was crossing. This was how, in 1784, the members of the Lodge of Saint Andrew, when called on to choose, decided to distinguish themselves from the conservative current of the Moderns. It is no accident that the Lodge of Saint Andrew recognized the first black lodge, which was created by the preacher and emancipated slave Prince Hall. (See color plate 2 for an image of Hall and his wife.) Hall had been initiated in 1775 by an Irish military lodge. In 1871 (after the Civil War) the Lodge of Saint Andrew vainly attempted to create another black lodge, the Thistle Lodge.

It can be seen that Freemasonry and the emerging American society were closely intertwined. Nevertheless, the War for Independence, as well as the later Civil War, revealed opposing currents that crossed through the lodges at the very time they were expanding rapidly. Also during this time, the itinerant military lodges played a role that should not be overlooked in the spread of Freemasonry. The arrival of British regiments on the East Coast of America after 1775 coincided with the flood of new lodges in the wake of the armies. With the organization of patriotic lodges triggered by the opening of the War for Independence, Freemasons also found themselves in the position of missionaries of the Order, but each on his own side and therefore at odds with the principle of the center of union formulated by Anderson. The most famous military lodge, without question, was that bearing the distinctively evocative sign of the American Union.

While this political and revolutionary context coincided with powerful tempests, it did not form any real hindrance to the effective establishment of Freemasonry or the activities of its lodges, which were visibly multiplying quite rapidly. This was also the case in the new territories opened by the Westward expansion, which too was accompanied by a noteworthy expansion of the Masonic presence.

Freemasonry, Founding "Establishment" and Power

The list of great American figures who were Freemasons at the very beginning of the United States is long—so long that a veritable cult of the founding fathers and their heritage is still practiced by the American grand lodges. The lodges were profoundly marked by the seal of patriotism, a worship of the flag, and the pledge of allegiance to the nation, as much as—but perhaps a little more intensely—than the civil society that was seeking to cohere around the key symbols of a new identity.

Of course, George Washington enjoys a preeminent position that none would dream of disputing in this pantheon of prestigious ancestors.

There is a wealth of literature and illustrations that depicts him in Masonic settings exercising his Masonic duties (see color plate 3 for one such image). The George Washington Masonic National Memorial of Alexandria, Virginia, near the gates of the federal capital, undeniably offers the most eloquent evidence of the veneration bestowed on him by American Freemasons. Built on a hilltop between 1910 and 1922, it is easily recognizable as an explicitly Masonic edifice. A monumental square and compass (some seventy feet long) were added to the front lawn to celebrate, where all could see, the brother and first leader of the American nation on the occasion of the two-hundredth anniversary of his death, June 26, 1999.

This memorial serves simultaneously as a showcase, a Masonic museum, an information center, and an archive. It also houses a large, active temple as well as the Masonic relics of Washington and Lafayette, another emblematic figure who is closely associated with this site. It is a building constructed on the model of the Alexandrian lighthouse, a symbol of the "times immemorial" from which the Masonic imagination draws its sustenance. It is impossible for visitors arriving at Ronald Reagan Washington National Airport not to see it. In a land of hyperboles, it is gladly introduced as "the most imposing Masonic building in the world."

The Bible on which Washington swore the oath during his inauguration as the first president of the United States on April 30, 1789, is a "Volume of the Sacred Law" that remains a highly esteemed object. Printed in London in 1765, this Bible is housed and displayed in the gallery of St. John's Lodge no. 1 at the Federal Hall National Memorial in New York. It's a veritable icon, and its high symbolic value remains so great even today that President Bill Clinton, like his successors George W. Bush and Barack Obama—none of whom are Freemasons—asked for and were granted its use when they took the oath of office. In the domain of iconography, the paintings and engravings depicting Brother George Washington in Masonic dress and setting the first stone of the Capitol—headquarters of Congress in Washington, D.C.—are legion.

Benjamin Franklin also appears among the number of particularly revered American Freemasons. The Benjamin Franklin National Memorial and the monument called the Signer in Philadelphia, where the independence of the United States was proclaimed on July 4, 1776, pays homage to the signers of the American Constitution. Their names and portraits are displayed, along with an indication that one-third of them were Freemasons. This is telling of how deep the origins of the United States were stamped by the seal of the Enlightenment and Masonic philosophy.

What we should see here is the extension of the extraordinary intellectual and scientific influence of the figures who were educated and trained in the tradition of excellence of London's Royal Society. But the part played by the French in American independence, at the forefront of which was the young general and brother Lafayette, was not of lesser standing. In this regard, the joint membership of Lafayette and Washington in the Masonic order was not without importance, as can be shown by the results of research. The Masonic museums of Alexandria and Philadelphia display Masonic aprons whose cartouches indicate that they belonged to Washington. One apron is even said to have been embroidered by Madame Lafayette herself. It is also said, however, that she assigned the task to nuns who piously crafted it. As is the case with many relics, the individuals capable of vouching for their authenticity must be quite knowledgeable as it seems there are many similar aprons elsewhere.

Today, despite what I just wrote about Lafayette, America's collective memory seems to have somewhat forgotten the major role played by the young French general in winning the independence of the United States; the young man took as his motto "For freedom to live, it will always require men to rise up and shake off indifference and resignation." Yet the fact remains that Lafayette is still a strong symbol of Franco-American ties. An exact replica of his ship, the *Hermione*, was built in Rochefort, France, and was sailed from France to the United States in 2015.

The construction of the replica of the *Hermione,* the frigate

Lafayette took in 1780 to come to America and join the colonial insurgents fighting for their independence, was undertaken in July 1997 by the Association Hermione-Lafayette in Rochefort to pay an authentic homage to Lafayette. This splendid and ambitious move seeks to preserve and bring to life the memory of a great adventure of solidarity between men; an adventure that fully conforms to the Masonic ideal. The Rochefort association, with legitimate pride, underscores this today, saying, "Rebuilding the *Hermione* is rebuilding an element of our maritime heritage. It is committing a large construction site to the betterment of the economy and culture of an entire region, because we need memory to build the future. Rochefort, a new city of the seventeenth century, owes its birth to Colbert's decision to establish a new arsenal for the kingdom of France on the banks of the Charente for the purpose of building, arming, supplying, and repairing a war fleet capable of withstanding enemy attacks."

Today, Rochefort is inventing itself a new future but is doing so by relying on its unique heritage. This heritage consists of the former Royal Rope Walks, restored after twenty years of effort and the jewel of the former arsenal, and the various dry docks, the oldest of which goes back to the eighteenth century. While the building of a replica of an eighteenth-century vessel fits into this reconquering of an identity, it also aims at providing France with evidence of its naval history as well as serving as a symbol of Franco-American fraternity through a ship that has attached its name to that of a man, Lafayette, a symbol of French support for the American revolutionaries. It is therefore also a duty of remembrance that involves the Freemasons of the GODF by not forgetting that Brother Lafayette was also a member of the Rochefort lodge.

Lafayette, Freemasonry, and American Independence

A number of reasons guided Lafayette's determined commitment to the cause of the American rebels. During this renowned Enlightenment

project to rebuild the frigate and in 2015 to retrace Lafayette's voyage to the United States, the American Friends of *Hermione*-Lafayette Association, paraphrased King's admirable expression as "We have a dream!"

We have seen the role played by the French Freemasons who contributed to the cause of liberty with Lafayette. But Washington was also surrounded by many Freemasons in the upper ranks of the military, and a good number of them distinguished themselves in the roles they played in the company of the father of independence. In his book *Masonic Membership of the Signers of the Declaration of Independence,* Ronald E. Heaton showed evidence that both the Declaration of Independence and the Articles of Confederation were signed by several Freemasons. However, it would be over the top to conclude from this that Freemasonry, in its capacity as an Order, would have taken on some institutional role. In fact, the preeminent position then held by Freemasons on an individual basis in the profane world could not hide another reality, one that pitted loyalists and rebels against one another, even within the lodges, which were not able to escape these irresistible forces.

It is helpful to know, however, that since independence, the United States has had no less than fourteen presidents who were Freemasons, the last one being Gerald Ford (see plate 4 in the color insert). This is something that at the least indicates, and in the most striking way, the actual presence of Freemasons in the highest positions of power in the nation until a relatively recent date and, also to the contrary, their absence at this level since the 1970s. This development has become the subject of scrutiny concerning the perennial nature of an involution-turning tradition that cannot fail to be translated as a loss of influence.

This is something that nonetheless remains relative when we understand where the true power centers reside in the United States. While the administration in power and the American president in particular have a significant arsenal at their disposal during their time in office, it is important, by the same token, not to overlook the power held by the members of Congress, whose growing influence can easily be seen during the most recent period of American politics. In both the House of Representatives and the Senate, Freemasons are still, even today, well represented and quite influential. To assert, as some do quite gladly when referring to the basic principles laid down by the grand lodges, that politics and Freemasonry don't mix does not stand up to analysis or is only accurate when referring to life in the lodge. Up to the present time in the United States any debate within the organization has been banned that involves any exchanges even touching on politics or religion—even in the broad sense.

This ban was caused as much by the tradition inherited from the United Grand Lodge of England as by the trauma induced by the Morgan Affair. (The details and consequences of this far-reaching scandal, the Morgan Affair, will be examined in chapter 3.) It remains no less established that a Masonic lobby exists in the same way as any other lobby that helps influence political, financial, economic, and social decisions in this vast country. Permeable circumstances do exist, unquestionably, even if America never experienced a situation comparable to that of France—in which the Order was set up at one time as a pedagogical laboratory for republican values.

Here we see again the weight of social ethnology specific to each country. Although coming from every latitude of common reference values, which no one would call the "fundamentals," Freemasonry finds itself shaped and modeled through adapting to its national environment. This plasticity does not always facilitate the reading of the Masonic order by those who measure it solely with what they are already most familiar; that is, their immediate environment—which necessarily shrinks their horizon.

At the Order's Origins
The United Lodge of England

At the Order's Origins,
Once upon a Time in London . . .

As the international Masonic world still bears the dominant brand of the Order's origins in London, it is inevitable that we need to look at the genesis, history, and characteristics of the United Grand Lodge of England such as they have been laid down. This involves recalling the reality of a very old institution with which all the world's Masonic authorities share the same original legacy. As recommended by Georges Lerbet and René Le Moal, "We shall not abandon ourselves to cheap reductionist notions."[1] This means, of course, that only the scientific method, the very same one applied by researchers and historians, allows an innovative approach of Masonic maieutics for drawing up a picture that restores—as precisely and closely as possible—the historical realities and their meanings.

The British cradle of our initiatory Order is evidence that continues to unfold some three hundred years later of the global supremacy of the United Grand Lodge of England, whose inner workings are worth analyzing. It is also worth attempting to place this into a contemporary perspective, as it is crucial for a proper appreciation of the forces that are present like axes around which the players gravitate. The overall

Masonic weight of London has been a dominating force for almost three centuries. While it is in decline today, it remains particularly visible on the American side of the Atlantic for reasons everyone will easily grasp, such as strong linguistic, cultural, and historical ties. American society has evolved considerably since the War of Independence and the arrival of successive waves of immigrants who passed through Ellis Island (the famous immigration center of New York).

All serious research studies push back the origins of Freemasonry, in the best of cases, to a Chester Lodge, whose existence is vouched for in the 1670s. Nonetheless, no serious proof has ever been put forth that can establish a connection between what the legal scholar, physician, and archaeologist Elias Ashmole mentioned in his 1682 journal and the founding of the four lodges of the Grand Lodge of London in 1717. It is therefore a good idea to interpret prudently the "awakening" mentioned by Anderson in his history, especially if the essential proof is not there. Freemasons are in agreement at least on one point, although simplified: all make reference to origins going back to "times immemorial."

As Florence de Lussy writes, "By giving themselves, from the time they became organized, a prestigious origin that goes back to the most remote time, by deliberately inscribing the new institution into a mythic context, they could not help but encourage among their historians, whether fervent adepts or detractors, a taste for half truths that engender and maintain confusion."[2] This occurred in the United States as it did everywhere else.

Everyone is familiar with the Reverend James Anderson, who was charged in 1723, with Jean Théophile Désaugliers, to codify the Order's rules and customs since its origin into what it is appropriate to call the *Constitutions,* a work that bears his name. They are the cornerstone of the first grand lodge of London. Every Freemason today still makes reference to them. The spiritual and philosophical influence of England in the European Masonic world since the beginning of the eighteenth century, then soon reaching America, is considerable, as is the grandeur of the extraordinary intellectual distinction of the prestigious English intelligentsia who were members of this first grand lodge.

Désaugliers, grand master of the Grand Lodge of England in 1719, a French Huguenot driven out of New Rochelle at a tender age following the repeal of the Edict of Nantes, was one of many great notables of a scientific and philosophical elite deeply marked by ties with John Locke and Isaac Newton, the latter a president of the Royal Society. Some forty of the two hundred members of this science academy were Freemasons, and twenty-one of them were grand masters of the Grand Lodge of London. The election of Désaugliers in 1714 as secretary of this prestigious scholarly society coincided with the Hanoverian succession crisis. He included in his entourage not only Ashmole but also the geometer and architect Christopher Wren, while his scientific collaborations brought him to France on several occasions and led to his meeting the German philosopher Gottfried Wilhelm Leibniz in London.

The effects of great mobility and the intense currents of exchange that were already flowing then were thus factors in the intermingling of ideas; these should not be overlooked when studying the precocious influence of the Grand Lodge of London. An essential stage in human emancipation, the emergence of English Freemasonry will remain as a major event in the evolution of societies. The lodge became the new framework for free thinking and a place for socializing in which men of different social status and convictions could mingle and, in the closed space of their meeting room, exercise their freedom of speech without constraint.

As François Thual writes, "For more than a century, British Masonry was being tugged between supporters of Stuart and those of Hanover. Since its origins, Freemasonry had always been divided within its organization into rival obediences."[3]

This reality, when all is said and done, has little to do with strictly doctrinal Masonic considerations but is precociously revealing of the interweaving of the political, the spiritual, and the Masonic in a ternary England that still rested (and did so until very recently) on the three major pillars of monarchy, church, and Masonry. The encounters of authority or the authorities with the Freemasons create a recurring theme that the denials of the English Freemasons, subsequently echoed by their American brothers, can do nothing to change.

It was Andreas Önnerfors, the former director of the Center of Masonic Studies at the University of Sheffield, who wrote in this regard.

> Two concepts of the Order appear. For the Anglo-Saxons, an associ- ation based on voluntary adherence was incompatible with a politi- cal role *sui generis,* but should be at the heart of a liberal concept of civil society. In France, to the contrary, with a more radical read- ing, Freemasonry identified itself as an active force for social, pro- gressive, and critical change, if not to say social engineering. This is why we can see two directions that are partially detectable since the eighteenth century: the one "esoteric" and resistant to revolutionary ideas, that finds common ground with the ideological powers of the Church and State, and the other that proactively pushes toward an "exoteric" realization of philanthropic ideas in conflict and in oppo- sition with the existing powers.
>
> On the individual level, the two ways come to bear, but differ- ently, on the choice of responsibility and on the nature of freedom. While the first direction regards ethical duty as the mainspring of the individual and Freemasonry's role in society is created by the sum total of the individual actions (*intra-muros*) morally assumed by the brothers, the more recent holds the individual as responsible for the liberation and transformation of society so that the political vir- tues cultivated in Freemasonry require by definition an *extra-muros* sociopolitical activity.
>
> Such a clear-cut distinction however is not applicable during all the decades of the century and not held as true for all the individ- uals that have subscribed to one or the other of these readings of Freemasonry. But it facilitates our understanding of the divergent positions and the notion of Freemasonry according to various politi-

cal cultures. And it helps us understand more clearly the difference between the various authoritative narratives, by taking into account the imaginal realm of the national communities and the construction of national identities that were such a pressing concern for the nineteenth century.[4]

This makes something quite obvious that would not be without consequence to the life of the Order in the United States: the Grand Lodge of London, like the United Grand Lodge of England after 1813, which was born of the reconciliation of the previously antagonistic currents of the Moderns and Ancients, recruited all its grand masters from the royal family. (The current grand master—since 1967—is none other than the Duke of Kent, with the executive office however belonging to the pro–grand master elected by his peers, who today is Derek Dinsmore.) The Grand Lodge has claimed since 1720 a worldwide predominance that is the expression of a political will translated by the codification of rules and basic principles, more commonly known as *Landmarks*. We can find them formulated already in Anderson's *Constitutions* in 1723, even if the chief objective of the author was most likely not yet the desire to establish a universal *doxa*. It is nonetheless true that the London leadership would impress itself in enduring fashion on the Masonic order, even though this position would be constantly challenged by the liberal Masonic currents, with the GODF being its principal rival and detractor.

But it is obvious that the stakes go beyond those of the Masonic sphere alone and touch, as everyone will easily understand, on the eternal competition between the two major powers of Britain and France. The obediences could not escape this. Pierre Mollier has said it best.

When in 1773, the Grand Orient of France succeeded the first Grand Lodge of France, . . . a fairly random correspondence had existed . . . with the Grand Lodge of England (of the "Moderns") since the 1760s. It even seems that an agreement had been signed in

1766 . . . and, since 1774, the English Grand Secretary and Deputy
Grand Master had been sounding the Grand Orient de France out
on its intentions concerning an international accord . . . which proposed to London a prospective treaty. . . . Based on the strict equality
of the signers, the Grand Lodge of England demanded that its primacy be recognized. . . . The Grand Orient of France refused to recognize any preeminence, even historical, to Grand Lodge of England
so because that lodge made this recognition a *sine qua non.* . . . The
great plan never came to fruition. The Grand Lodge of England, or
its successor, the United Grand Lodge of England, and the Grand
Orient of France would therefore never maintain official relations.

Mollier goes on to write:

When questioned on the reasons that led the GODF to refuse to
accept . . . something that was yet patently obvious, when this mini-
mal concession would have in no way limited its independence or
sovereignty, we should probably refer back to the context of the era.
The French defeat at the hands of England in the Seven Years War
(1756–1763, cf. *Barry Lyndon*) had left a bitter taste. The 1770s
saw the emergence in France of a patriotic sentiment of which, to a
certain extent, the creation of the Grand Orient of France was the
Masonic translation. This national sentiment and its direct consequence, revenge on England, would be stimulated from 1774 on by
the "war in America." The refusal of England's Masonic primacy,
although self-evident, is probably the echo of the refusal to accept
England's colonial supremacy.[5]

By instituting Landmarks that would be repeatedly updated and
revised, as a constant strategy to ensure dominance over the universal space of Masonry, London strove, with admirable consistency, to
develop its pragmatic and dogmatic doctrine. These actions were solidly influenced by London's obvious concern for preserving its private

garden, to such an extent that it is not too exaggerated to find an analogy between it and the papal bull of Pope Clement XII, *In eminenti*. In fact, the grand lodges recognized by London were obliged, at the risk of their excommunication, along with that of their members, to submit without any concession to the canons enacted in the form of Landmarks. The first adaptations to these Landmarks were made in 1929, and they have been tailored several times since then in response to geopolitical fluctuations, as so splendidly analyzed by Marius Lepage.

In the dialectic of the United Grand Lodge of England, this posture assumes a dual meaning: the recognition of a grand lodge is conditional on a catalogue of stipulations that has nothing to do with Masonic initiation; this latter notion, moreover, does not exist in English and American Freemasonry, where the individual candidate simply makes his "entry." One of these conditions—one that is politically essential—stipulates that only one obedience can benefit from that status in a given country. London thereby assumes the exclusive prerogative of writing the law by boasting its precedence going back to 1717, a historical fact that nobody contests.

The exclusivity that derives from this is quite another matter, one that is of course another source of contention. The fact remains that it is a time-proven, dreadfully effective diplomatic tool to establish and install one's empire in a rule that is practically undivided, as long as the others consent. In this way any form of Masonic heresy (meaning deviation from any Landmark) that may arise to disrupt this sterilized environment that attests to fine doctrinal certitudes can be expelled. But in practice, a dent had already been made in this rule of exclusive jurisdiction, most importantly since the recognition of the African American Prince Hall Grand Lodge. The opening of this breech had obviously prompted covetousness—as well as speculations, most unexpectedly in France.

Two essential principles of the Landmarks of September 4, 1929, are worth lingering over momentarily: regularity and its corollary, irregularity, as criteria for recognition are formed from whole cloth, and none of the foundational texts ever mentioned them. For instance, the basic principles as formulated by Anderson in the 1723 *Constitutions* did not possess the constraining nature that is attached to the *fundamental principles* of the United Grand Lodge of England. The criteria London used in the definition of the Landmarks emphasized the specific history of the Ancients, who had retained as their three sources of wisdom the Bible (renamed *Volume of the Sacred Law*), the square, and the compass. This was, however, without taking into account the first tradition, that of the Moderns, for whom the three great lights at the origin of the Order were the sun, the moon, and the elder master in the lodge, which would have rendered the coercive exercise somewhat more complex.

In passing we see there the geopolitical interlinking of elements of obediential doctrine and strategies. The earliest sources of the doctrine that was gradually conceived and established by the United Grand Lodge of England in the form of metarules only date, by the way, from 1809. As Lepage strove to show in the footsteps of Henry Sadler, it was the Lodge of Promulgation that during this year undertook a codification, starting with the fixing of two restrictive rules for the ceremonies for installing their masters.[6] What followed in 1929 was of an entirely different nature and aimed at determining the criteria that authorized London to declare an obedience as regular or irregular, which is to say to maintain its tight control.

At the end of the nineteenth century the American Albert Mackey had already attempted to establish (and was the first to do so) an extensive catalog of twenty-five Landmarks, a veritable dogmatic set, published in his *An Encyclopedia of Freemasonry*. It was therefore by a very gradual process that the United Grand Lodge of England equipped itself with a new body of texts, the *Aims and Relationships of the Crafts*, written in 1929, then amended in August 1938 and again in 1949. The last revisions were made in 1989. Spencer Douglas David Compton, Lord Northampton, former pro–grand master of the London obedience and considered to be a liberal authority—who has since been replaced by a more conservative successor—set the doctrine by interpreting it as follows:

> Several obediences can be considered to be regular in each country or region. It is not the responsibility of the United Grand Lodge of England to prejudge as the prerogative of recognition belonging to the obedience recognized by London, and it is up to the Masonic authorities concerned to find agreement among themselves.
>
> Recognition by a recognized obedience in no way implies recognition on the part of the United Grand Lodge of England.
>
> Consequently, an obedience recognized by the United Grand Lodge of England keeps the latitude of recognizing obediences that are not recognized by the United Grand Lodge of England.

This recent development is evidence of a new plasticity in the system of recognition that takes nothing away from the primacy of the United Grand Lodge of England, whereas each of the preceding texts had restricted a little more each time the freedom of contact with the liberal obediences, designated with much condescension and sometimes proscribed outright. Those who remember the twists and turns surrounding the Alpina Grand Lodge in the 1960s will recall the shock waves caused by the English policy concerning obediences in continental Europe, particularly in Germany and France. In this way, the United Grand Lodge of England, in a belated doctrinal reorientation, unilaterally maintains the arrangements determining recognition by imposing the norms of regularity, all while recently introducing a more subtle dialectic that on the whole is most pragmatic.

It remains no less established that American Masonry, long under the grip of the doctrine formulated by the United Grand Lodge of England, fit itself into this caesura between the two Masonic trends that developed as they drew ever further away from each other. The session of the Grand Lodges Conference at Baltimore, Maryland, in February 2014 offered confirmation of the *qua* eternal contortions of Franco-American interactions in this domain. I would like to cite the report that appeared in the blog "La Lumière" by the journalist François Koch in *L'Express*.

> The Grand Master of the GLNF (25,000 brothers), Jean-Pierre Servel, pronounced himself "satisfied" with his visit to Baltimore where he attended the Conference of the North American Grand Masters from February 15–18, 2014, in the state of Maryland on the East Coast of the United States. This large annual gathering officially claims representation of some two million masons and sixty Grand Lodges belonging to the United States (including Washington, D.C., and Puerto Rico), Mexico, Canada, as well as incidentally the American-Canadian Grand Lodge of Germany that was created after the Second World War in the former occupied zones. In 2014, the French question was brought before the Commission on Information for Recognition, with the interventions of not just one advocate for the cause but both protagonists of the structures created by the crisis of the GLNF in 2013, Allain Juillet (grand master of the Grande Loge de l'Alliance Maçonnique Française [GLAMF]) and Jean-Pierre Servel (grand master of the GLNF).[7]

Servel was asked the following three questions by Koch.

Why were you satisfied?

Because the Commission on Information for Recognition, which, in 2012, had deemed it reasonable to "suspend relations with the GLNF," has changed its position: "Considering the resolution of administrative problems, the member Grand Lodges can, if they so desire, reconsider this suspension. This is positive for us. All the same, you should know that we are not starting from zero: out of

51 American Grand Lodges, we are recognized by 35 (by an additional 4 over the past two years).

Is the return of English recognition anticipated to be soon?

I am quite hopeful of this. I spoke at length with the Grand Chancellor of the United Grand Lodge of England (Derek Dinsmore). What the English wish is for peace to be restored and for the brothers to be happy. In Baltimore we showed a pacified Masonry, without permanent war.

What are the consequences for French Masonry?

I have never said that the GNLF should remain the sole regular obedience in France. If one or more strictly respect the Landmarks (belief in God, the rule of no Masonic intervisits with irregular Masonic entities . . .), I am favorable to joining together in a confederation or within the United Grand Lodges.

Meanwhile Juillet, grand master of the GLAMF (with seventeen thousand members), which was born from the scission of the GLNG in 2013, was already betting on a confederation of French Masonry bringing together some seventy thousand brothers with a strategy based on the Declaration of Vienna of January 2014 (see the appendices). This declaration was written by five European grand lodges, with the United Grand Lodge of Germany being the most passionate of the militants for the cause and consequently seen as the leader.

What we are seeing here are the sudden jolts of institutions seeking an exit and in quest of recognition and therefore international legitimacy in an eternal Franco-American interaction, as well as, in some way, a drift of Masonic continents henceforth separated by abysses.

The grand masters of the grand lodges of North America and their Commission on Information for Recognition, for their part, defined the standards this way in 1952:

Legitimacy of origin, in other words, when going back to their historical sources: what obedience provided their charter?

Exclusive territorial jurisdiction, exceptions made by mutual agreement and/or treaty;

Adherence to the old Landmarks—more specifically: belief in God; the *Volume of the Sacred Law* forms an essential and constituent part of the lodge, and the taboo on political or religious discussions.

It was therefore on these criteria that obediences in trans-Atlantic, or more generally, international, relations were either recognized or not. However, the commission today explicitly states that it communicates this information for their use by the grand lodges "with no intention of influencing or recommending the actions they would wish to be taken." This is a theoretically more liberal reading than that of the United Grand Lodge of England, which thereby leaves some virtual maneuvering room for each obedience, on condition of respecting one doxa at minimum. The future will say what practical consequences will be drawn from this and how they will be judged by the measure of actual recognitions.

With regard to the United Grand Lodge of England in London, even with the belated softening agreed to lessen the pressure of realities, it has imposed its Landmarks in a way that is both lasting and quite effective. Respect for these Landmarks is required of the regular grand lodges, in the sense this Masonic authority is interpreted. American standards are therefore an interpretative application of English norms. The obediences in this circle of influence meet every two years in international conferences organized by each member lodge in turn, in regional or continental alternation.

This international network currently contains 246 grand lodges worldwide, which breaks down to 107 in North America, 68 in Latin America, 43 in Europe, 17 in Africa, and 11 in the Asian Pacific region. Furthermore, the leadership of the United Grand Lodge of England mainly manifests as external policies coordinated with the American network, reaching wherever it is deemed necessary and especially helpful for the penetration of this Masonic network into new areas. In Central and Eastern Europe after the fall of the Berlin Wall in 1989, and in Russia and its former satellites after they were opened in 1991, the creation of grand lodges in this circle of influence multiplied without the lodges necessarily always being successfully established.

These activities were led with the openly displayed support of the Commission on Information for Recognition of the Grand Lodges of the United States of America, and they obviously obeyed a geostrategic and diplomatic philosophy. The unacknowledged but established political links with missions serving American interests are obvious and even publically notorious, because they involve ensuring external relays suitable to serving the higher causes of the empire. So there will be no cause for surprise upon learning of the generosity that benefited those who took as their mission the formation of grand lodges in the countries of the former Eastern bloc. In this respect, we shall see in chapter 7 how when the interests of the Supreme Council of France entered into conflict with those of the Southern Jurisdiction in 1995, this mirrored exactly the competition between the French and the American nations.

This was the resounding expression of what was aimed for here. And, sticking with the theme of geopolitical realities, it should come as no surprise that Russian president Vladimir Putin chose to join in a philosophy of reciprocal support with the Russian obedience of the Grand Orient of the Russian Peoples.

The American Spiritual
Infusion and Freemasonry

Ethnology, Sociology, and Evolutions

To better understand American Freemasons, it is important to take into consideration the sociocultural context in which they have lived and evolved since the beginning of their short history. In fact, their markers and reference points are fairly different in many respects from those of their continental European brethren, especially those of Mediterranean cultures. This is truly the case despite the common sources from which Freemasons on both sides of the Atlantic draw. Since their beginnings, the first North American lodges incontestably bore the mark of the extremely singular context of New England, which some have outfitted with a very specific name that means exactly what it purports to mean: WASP (white Anglo-Saxon Protestant).

The spiritual filiation of Pastor James Anderson, author of the *Constitutions* of Freemasonry, is undeniably interpreted with a zest, or added touch, of Protestantism that is quite different from the thought that prevails in Europe. This Christian spiritualist mind-set may be even more accentuated and underscored in light of the famous Morgan Affair, which we shall examine later in this chapter and which took place in nearby New York State in 1826 and left behind profound impressions. In a country whose motto is "In God we trust," identifying oneself as a freethinker is poorly viewed, even today. This can be an inconceivable incongruity in the mind of an American Freemason, for whom the Great Architect, a notion of intangible reference, can be nothing other than God—a revealed god, in all cases. Secularism itself is a notion that is foreign to the American universe and, consequently, is quite difficult for the normally educated mind of the average United States' citizen to imagine.

A poll taken at the beginning of the year 2001 by the Pew Research Center is quite significant in this regard. Seventy percent of the individuals questioned felt it was important for them that the president of the United States have religious convictions, whereas even the United States Constitution guarantees the separation of church and state. It is, moreover, because of the First Amendment guaranteeing the absolute freedom of religious practice, a legacy of the *Mayflower,* that this nation has such a profusion of sects and tiny religious groups of all sorts, more than anywhere else in the world.

This is displayed most notably by the proliferation of religious buildings, which also confirms the dominance of a consubstantial spirituality in America and which is in such sharp contrast with Europe that it cannot help but surprise visitors from the Old World. In this regard, it is also significant that 45 percent of the people questioned in that same 2001 poll stated that they attended a religious service at least once a week. However, American society is, by definition, dynamic; another poll taken in 2011 revealed that at that time almost one out of four Americans admitted that they did not believe in any god.

By considering all these elements, it is easier to see that Freemasonry and a variety of religions get along rather well in the United States. But, as nothing is ever simple, the relations of the Order with some ecclesiastical institutions are worth examining and are required for a more accurate evaluation. The debate on the separation of church and state figures, in a completely different way than in France, into the agenda of the causes certain Masons defend. The principle behind this appears evident in the museum of the Southern Jurisdiction of the Ancient and Accepted Scottish Rite in Washington, D.C.

The analysis of what distinguishes American religious spirituality and that of the United States' Freemasons is so essential that it is crucial to devote several substantive assessments, backed up by citations from famous Freemasons, to this topic. Faith in God and the obligation to refer to a revealed deity are of such capital importance in American Masonic tradition that they form the veritable pivot around which Masonic doctrine revolves in this region. It therefore comes as no surprise that Albert Pike gave his major work of Masonic teaching the title *Morals and Dogmas.* One of the other best-known theoreticians of American Freemasonry, Albert Mackey, was also the author in the mid-nineteenth century of important reference works that still command authority today, such as his *Lexicon of Freemasonry* and his *Symbolism of Freemasonry.*

In 1908, Arthur Preuss analyzed this situation in his book *Étude sur la Franc-maçonnerie américaine* to cast "more light on American Freemasonry as a religion." In chapter 4, we find this:

> The idea of introducing Masonry as religion must appear so novel to a good many of our readers and the protests it will inspire will be so vociferous and prolonged that a little light shed on this matter will not be out of place. Let us allow Dr. Mackey to take the trouble to instruct us. . . : "There has been a needless expenditure of ingenuity and talent, by a large number of Masonic orators and essayists, in the endeavor to prove that Masonry is not religion. This has undoubtedly arisen from a well-founded but erroneous view that has been taken of the connection between religion and Masonry, and from a fear that if the complete disseverance of the two was not made manifest, the opponents of Masonry would be enabled successfully to establish a theory that they have been fond of advancing, that the Masons were disposed to substitute the teachings of their Order for the truths of Christianity.
>
> "Now I have never," he adds, "for a moment believed that any

such unwarrantable assumption, as that Masonry is intended to be a substitute for Christianity, could ever obtain admission into any well-regulated mind, and, therefore, I am not disposed to yield, on the subject of the religious character of Masonry, quite so much as has been yielded by more timid brethren. On the contrary I contend, without any sort of hesitation, that Masonry is, in every sense of the word, except one, and that its least philosophical, an eminently religious institution—that it is indebted solely to the religious element that it contains for its origin and for its continued existence, and that without this religious element it would scarcely be worthy of cultivation by the wise and good. But, that I may be truly understood, it will be well first to agree upon the true definition of religion. . . ." This piety that could accommodate itself to any notion of God would be strange.[1]

And Preuss concludes by underscoring the reference to a revealed deity in that "this is sufficient proof that Masonry is not only religion, but it is clearly a religion," a hypothesis he would develop more fully and strongly backed by supporting arguments drawn from American Masonic literature.

In chapter 18, he then asks:

Does American Masonry in fact form one entity with European Masonry? It is to be regretted . . . that this simple question has too often garnered equally simple answers, with no attention given to the fact that the same words can have very different meanings. The affirmative, just like the negative, is thereby exposed to serious difficulties. If one is dealing with a Catholic, if he refuses to accept that the identity of Masonry in Europe and the identity of Masonry in America are definitely two different things, it will be difficult for him to defend the procedures of his church that rejects all Masons without distinction . . . and excommunicate all American Masons, just like their European brethren. If, to the contrary, he asserts the identity of the two Masonries, he will inspire a storm of protests from Masons and non-Masons alike, and place himself in the position of having to explain the difference of mind and behavior that seems to exist between the two bodies of Masonry, with that of the continent being a fervent adversary of Catholicism, which is not the case with American Masonry. If both are one entity, how are we then to explain this difference?[2]

It could be tempting to expect that ways of thinking have evolved since the beginning of the twentieth century and to extrapolate the effects of secularization that can be seen almost everywhere in Europe into twenty-first-century America. But this is not the case whatsoever. Even while some obediences of the Old World have maintained the traditional obligatory evocation of the Great Architect of the Universe—which is the freely chosen case in more than a hundred lodges of all rites in the GODF—it is not at all a reference to a revealed god; there is still the longstanding difference with the American lodges, in which God is always placed at the pinnacle of Masonic philosophical thought.

This remains such a sensitive subject today that it continues to be the subject of booklets and position papers. For example, two high American Masonic officials of the Supreme Council of the Southern Jurisdiction of the Ancient and Accepted Scottish Rite, Arturo de Hoyos and S. Brent Morris, devoted a book, published in 1997 by the Masonic Information Center, to this topic under the title *Is It True What They Say about Freemasonry?* In it we find, in the domain of religion, a refutation by one of the authors in response to one of the Order's detractors. "Masonry is not my religion; Jesus is infinitely more important to me than the lodge. I have studied the Bible more than the Masonic ritual. . . . In fact, it was through the Masonic ritual that I became interested in studying the Bible."[3]

This is a response that is difficult to imagine in Europe, including in the regular lodges. It quite simply reveals a certain American reality. However, the nature and the editorial origin of these writings leave no doubt as to their "authorized" nature.

The Morgan Affair and
the Anti-Masonic Movement

If there is any well-known episode that speaks to the twists and turns of the Masonic order in the United States of America, it would be the Morgan Affair of 1826 (whose details remain murky to most) above all others. Yet the scandal (this is clearly a case where the word is appropriate), inspired by the mysterious disappearance of William Morgan, was so resounding that the shockwave it produced is still echoing almost two centuries later.

What was the nature of this scandal? Everything appears to have been started by a mundane announcement of the divulgence of the "secrets of Freemasonry." There had been quite a few earlier ones, mainly Samuel Prichard's famous *Masonry Dissected,* published in London in 1730. That was soon followed by a French translation in Paris. Such a divulgence was far from being an isolated action in the United States, as Hoyos has recently pointed out in his introduction to the reissue of his *Light on Masonry.* It is also helpful in this context to make reference to the reprinting in 1730 of *The Mystery of Freemasonry,* published by Benjamin Franklin himself. (Those familiar with Franklin's extremely eccentric itinerary know that he was a renowned publisher before going on to a brilliant future as a politician, philosopher, scientist, and diplomat.) Later in his life, Franklin would also become venerable master of the famous Lodge of the Nine Sisters in Paris.

Let us put the importance of the action for which William Morgan was accused in absolute perspective. When he made the announcement in Batavia, New York, in 1826 that an imminent publication was in preparation on the secrets and practices of Freemasonry, he nevertheless did not take into account a religious, social, and political context that was quite different from the one in which the spirited Franklin had acted without arousing the slightest dismay.

In 1798, two books condemning an alleged Masonic conspiracy had brought more grist to the mill of the adepts of this theory: *Proofs of a Conspiracy against All the Religions and Governments of Europe* by the British writer John Robinson and *Mémoires illustrant l'histoire du Jacobinisme* (Memoirs Illustrating the History of Jacobinism) by Abbé Barruel, a former French Jesuit. These publications left nothing to chance. They fell into a post-1789 antirevolutionary offensive that tended to lend credence to the theory of a conspiracy hatched by the Illuminati of Adam Weishaupt, who was accused of having infiltrated the Masonic lodges. Both Robinson and Barruel raised the standards of throne and altar to put people on their guard against the threat they anticipated would soon emerge in all lands, a threat posed by the apostles of equality, liberty, and popular sovereignty. To prop up their theory of a Masonic conspiracy, Robinson and Barruel made the case that Weishaupt, a professor of canon law at the University of Ingolstadt in Germany, through the Order of the Illuminati, taught the "precepts of resistance to the authority of the state, promising to destroy ecclesiastical power."

The echoes these assertions found first in the Protestant religious circles of the United State helped forge an even greater authentic, primordial alliance between freedom and religion that had already existed in this country. Since the heroic era of the *Mayflower,* religion has been deeply inscribed within the genes of American political and social life. American religious thought is therefore consubstantial to this society, which did not follow the same paths as European society. There, the Encyclopedists in France and Immanuel Kant in Königsberg, Germany, initiated the separation between religion and society, whereas across the Atlantic, although a formal separation between church and state existed, God was never declared dead and was never entirely absent from public debate. It so happens that these revelations, mixed with deeply felt speculations, demonized the "enemies of the altar and the throne" by identifying them as minions of Satan, cosmopolitan individuals without faith or law, subversive traitors, and promoters of moral anarchy. Suffice it to say that the Puritan Calvinists who emigrated to America, their new Promised Land, could not help but be receptive to this kind of propaganda. Their Catholic counterparts did not lag long behind them in this respect.

The mistake made by William Morgan and his publisher, David Miller, who had certainly been initiated into Masonry but never moved beyond the grade of apprentice, was, most likely and primarily, to have not realized that the context had changed and that the timing of their undertaking was particularly ill chosen. Both men appear to have been, in the eyes of many historians, essentially motivated by the lure of immediate profit. Morgan had such a shady reputation personally that he easily inspired some distrust.

Morgan's Masonic initiation is still a source of questions, as there remains no trace of its having ever occurred. Some venture the hypothesis that he may have been received into a lodge in Canada then peddled his knowledge of the rituals he had learned by heart by becoming an itinerant tutor—in return for money—in the service of the lodges. Contrary to some theories that tend to denigrate Morgan's abilities, his intellectual capacities, his memory in any case, do not appear to be the subject of any doubt, as opposed to his ethics. He is believed to have even acquired an excellent and encyclopedic mastery of the entire corpus of the Order's rituals.

Freemasons, staggered as much by Morgan's candor as by his greed, for that was perhaps his primary motivation, attempted to buy the manuscript. This was a wasted effort. This is the point where everything becomes complicated and the reading of the true motivations of Morgan and his publisher become unclear. If greed alone was the foundation of their undertaking, why then did they refuse to surrender the manuscript? From this point, focus was placed on questions concerning their desire to harm the Masonic order and on possible sponsors of their plan for new divulgences.

The house of Miller, the publisher, was set on fire several times. This is a clue that is hardly deceptive and would become a fairly legitimate source of suspicion. "Who benefits from the crime?" we could ask. Those who know America well will not be surprised by the methods applied in a society that still often carries the mark of the pioneers, accustomed to bullying those who for one reason or another are forming an obstacle to their designs. A society that knows, perhaps more than any other, the primacy of violence when it involves ensuring that one's "rights" prevail. This concept is key to the success of the extremely powerful National Rifle Association, which, against all democratic humanist logic, defends the absolute right of gun ownership. They advocate this so fiercely that no candidate for president dares confront them. The Democrat Barack Obama was no exception.

Without simplifying things too greatly, we see this tendency in the violent expulsion of the Indians during the winning of the West, the never-solved assassination of John F. Kennedy, and George W. Bush's war in Iraq. It is a cultural thing, the experts will glibly say, and the history of a country where "all is possible"—the best, as the historic election of former president Obama reminds us, and the worst—a country that is teeming with examples both inside and out. It is not an insult to America or Americans to make this observation.

From this to concluding in this instance that Freemasons would have been the arsonists, it is only a step that some refuse to take, allowing for a reasonable doubt. Conversely, some suspect David Miller of having counted on this and used it to inspire an unhealthy notoriety that would aid the commercialization of the book, promising to make it a sensation . . . and profitable.

Morgan, opportunely prosecuted by one of his creditors, in this instance the elder of the lodge of Canandaigua, New York, was condemned for an unfortunate two-dollar debt and found himself in prison on September 11, 1826. The next day, the complainant, Nicolas Chestero, accompanied by several Freemasons, went to the prison, where he withdrew his complaint. Restored to liberty, Morgan was abducted on the spot by a small squad of Freemasons who were obviously little prone to displaying any excessive feelings of fraternity. Witnesses said they heard William Morgan shouting, "Help!" and even, "Murder!" which is at least probable. Indeed, one author, Mac Coil, believes that Morgan was taken to a destination in the north of the state of New York, where he was sequestered until September 19. All trace of Morgan was lost after this date. However, an unidentified corpse was recovered on October 7, 1827, some thirteen months later, near Fort Niagara. The judicial and police investigations ended by classifying the file as closed with no further action. His widow would, however, identify the body of her unfortunate spouse much later, under improbable circumstances that were too providential not to have been staged and are therefore contestable, to say the least.

It required nothing more, given the context described earlier, for this disappearance to unleash a vast anti-Masonic campaign. The Order's detractors had only been waiting for a golden opportunity like this. While New York State had 480 lodges in 1826, the groundswell would leave behind only seventy-five in 1835, and the three supreme councils of the Ancient and Accepted Scottish Rite that had then been coexisting ceased all activity. But social and political authorities displayed an equal indignation—whether real, sham, or requested. Both the religious and the most conservative circles found in this mysterious disappearance a pretext for attacking the presumed occult power of the Masonic order in its entirety.

The question was asked: How could the president and Freemason Andrew Jackson and the American government tolerate an occult power, a state within a state—in this instance Freemasonry—that was targeted by an accusing finger, even if the accusations were not supported by any material proof? This denial of justice was considered an affront to the popular will. The popular conception was that the Order would have had no hesitation about "eliminating those who thwarted its dark designs." The moment had therefore arrived for religious circles to condemn Freemasonry for its anti-Christian attitude, for which it was labeled now more than ever. The term *anti-Christian* had been set loose. So much so that from New England to the Midwest we witnessed for the first time in American history the emergence, next to two major parties, of a third new, large political party: the Anti-Masonic Party.

Starting in 1827, a clamor arose for demoting Freemasons from public office, and the anti-Masonic wave was frequently accompanied by acts of physical violence. The Grand Lodges of Ohio and Pennsylvania were ordered to turn over their archives as well as all their documents to the civil authorities, and public officials were given the duty of searching the premises.

However, this campaign would wane after about a decade, but only after the party had proved beneficial to several well-known politicians. This included former American president John Quincy Adams as well as Millard Fillmore, who would become the thirteenth occupant of the White House in the near future. By the mid-1830s, many of the party's members had been absorbed into the new Whig Party. Still, the political earthquake triggered by the Morgan Affair is comparable in many pertinent ways to the anti-Communist witch hunt engineered by U.S. senator Joseph McCarthy after the end of the Second World War with the powerful support of the Christian right.

It is enough to surf the Web to become convinced of the durable nature of the theory of the Masonic conspiracy, to which certain Internet sites still devote themselves today by diving in to the phantasmagorical world fueled by and around the Morgan Affair. Televangelist Pat Robertson was doing nothing less in 1991 when he published his assertions on a *new world order* that resurrected the idea of a Freemason conspiracy, which was supposed to be confirmed by the presence of French brothers on the Trilateral Commission.

It was these periodic resurgences of the prolonged effects of the Morgan Affair that finally convinced Hoyos and Morris to publish the book I mentioned earlier titled *Is It True What They Say about Freemasonry?* This publication is testimony to their desire to counter not only the lasting, adverse effects of the Morgan Affair but also those from the most unbridled delusions.

Denis Lacorne, a great expert on religion in America, has devoted a book to this subject, *De la religion en Amérique,* in which he continually makes reference to "the sometimes astute but more often biased outlook of the French, seduced by the exoticism of an America so foreign to their national tradition and ways of thinking." For the outside observer in Europe, and for the French one in any case, several observations are called for here.

As I have already had the opportunity to write, this affair has had nothing but negative consequences from the perspective of the Masonic order and its place in American society. As the accusations targeting the Order have never been backed up, Freemasons can consider themselves absolved by benefit of the doubt. No archive, no document, nor any prosecution testimony has been kept that might give credit to the accusations. Cleared of these slanderous suspicions, American Freemasons have recovered their luster in one of those bursts of momentum so typical of an American culture that believes all things are possible, including the most improbable exploits.

Alexis de Tocqueville taught us this reading of an America, which we can also find with these characteristics, of course, in Freemasonry. Certainly for a French Freemason of any obedience, as well as for many European Freemasons, American Masonic practice can appear strange. It essentially remains in a position of sociability that proscribes any in-depth debate that might prove divisive inside the lodge. But we need only read what is still being published in the United States today to find convincing evidence of the serious approach taken by the researchers toiling on the study of this legacy of our common origins.

American Freemasonry today can assert itself confidently and assume a visibility that no longer need fear the persecutions that followed on the heels of the Morgan Affair. The American Masonic order happily identifies with the higher institutional interests of the United States and runs no risk—far from it—of being accused of cosmopolitanism. Its sociology assuredly gives it safe haven. It is imperial, if not a party of imperialism, and still assertively recognizes itself in emblematic figures like the former president and Freemason James Monroe, father of the famous dictum "America for the Americans" and of the Monroe Doctrine, which made him a contestable figure in Latin America, or even FBI Director J. Edgar Hoover, organizer of the most despicable works of McCarthyism and a figure of fear, even for those in his entourage. Hoover and McCarthy were both main players in one of the less glorious episodes in American history, known as the "red scare," which lasted from 1947 to 1953.

This was a period of inquisitional proceedings led by McCarthy's commission that hunted down—with the support of the FBI—possible Communist agents, militants, or suspects and sought just as hard to reduce the expression of political or social opinions it deemed suspect by restricting civil rights on the pretext of defending national security. By comparison, at this time, when the world is upset by the revelations of a renegade who showed the practices of the National Security Agency and its governmental program of international espionage and surveillance to the entire world, the whistleblower Edward Snowden pales in comparison.

But let's take precautions against falling into the easy snare of generalizations and judgments spun from whole cloth, and let's refrain from reducing American Masonry based on the actions of McCarthy and Hoover or even being too quick to bury a major body of the universal Masonic order that still has a wealth of resources and is quick to regenerate, as all recent signs are proving. After a vertiginous decline in the number of members and the alarming aging of those who remained, American Freemasonry has definitely initiated a substantial rebound worthy of what the world is accustomed to expect from this country, with its extraordinary ability to meet any challenge.

We should never lose sight of the fact that this great nation is also a polymorphous land of contrasts that never fails to surprise. The catharsis produced by the Morgan Affair certainly is not enough to explain the rebound, but it is part of it. At the same time, no one will ever understand the deist anchoring of American Freemasons without becoming aware of their perseverant efforts to lay it on even thicker in this regard since the Morgan Affair; although the omnipresence, if not the primacy, of a civil religion uniting quite varied beliefs, the national messianism, and the taste—including among Freemasons—for prayer are all equally significant cultural markers of American society. They do not even have to overdo it. If there are philosophical domains that separate the French from the Americans by a considerable distance, this is most likely one of them.

Lastly, belief combines with the redeeming mission of the American "New Jerusalem," the dream of a better future for humanity—one that is undeniably religious. This is what William James endeavored to conceptualize by his hypothesis reconciling pragmatism and religion.[4] This is a philosophical approach to which most if not almost all American Masons of all generations adhere. So it forms no obstacle to the possible adhesion of the American generations rising to an understanding of the Masonic order that remains foreign, if not downright strange, to the French.

We are dealing with two different societal notions. And while the Morgan Affair undeniably had aftereffects, it was clearly in this domain of a relationship with the Great Architect of the Universe that there became a kind of Masonic nonnegotiable dogma. Inside the Order, it is still being expanded upon with doctrinal positions that are just as intangible as the principles arising out of the 1877 Congress for the Freemasons of GODF regarding absolute freedom of conscience. In both cases history combines the spiritual construction of the Order with attempts to shape, *in fine,* doctrinal points that are difficult to reconcile but are thereby not designed to oppose each other if each individual accepts this "difference with the other that, far from wounding, enriches," to paraphrase the writer and aviator Antoine de Saint-Exupéry.

In another vein, one of the best examples that can be presented to illustrate the gulf that separates our two spheres in many respects is the eternal debate on the individual right to bear arms, recently illustrated by the wall of unyielding resistance into which Barack Obama collided throughout his presidency. The rate of gun deaths in the United States is around thirty thousand a year according to a study released by the Brady Campaign to Prevent Gun Violence, which includes homicides, suicides, and accidental deaths. According to the FBI, there were 8,583 murders by firearm in 2011, an average of twenty-three a day. When the American president displayed his firm intention to legislate an end to the serial massacres taking place in schools and public places, he ran into stiff opposition from Congress.

The part played by Republican and Freemason legislators is not insignificant. There is no real cause for surprise here, because the gun lobby, which claims more than four million supporters, equal to less than 1.5 percent of the population, exercises undeniable power over American politics. It is closely connected with American Masonic circles and the National Rifle Association, which fiercely campaigns against any restrictions on the right to bear arms. The pro-gun lobby also benefits from the favorable opinion of 68 percent of Americans.

This context deserves consideration, and it is thus necessary to know that, while proclaiming ethical principles, the same individuals refuse to consider any reform in this area, even though in a land of 318 million inhabitants there are no less than 300 million firearms in circulation, an average of almost one gun per inhabitant. In reality, these pistols, revolvers, assault rifles, and hunting guns bring happiness to 42 million homes; in other words, *only* 40 percent of American households. According to a study carried out by the Boston University School of Public Health, the right of gun ownership is supported by 57.7 percent of the U.S. population. Gun culture is, therefore, deeply anchored, and the reservations about any form of gun control are many, as shown by the recent recall of two Colorado senators who had supported making the law tougher.

What credibility can the speech on the special place of Freemasonry as a rampart for the defense of values, heard at the Conference of Grand Lodges in Baltimore, truly enjoy under these conditions? This really raises the question.

Masonry, Churches, and Sects

We have seen that the spirituality of American Freemasons, which is essentially religious and has little in common with the cerebral exercise in which the Freemasons who present engraved plates in the French Masonic tradition indulge, as more broadly do those of continental Europe. In the temples of American lodges this anaesthetizing method assures peace and serenity as it is still forbidden here to broach any subject that might prompt debate, but it makes the contemplative exercise nigh incomprehensible to anyone accustomed to a fruitful exchange strictly regulated by the presiding venerable master assisted by the two wardens. In American lodges, everything is perfectly sterilized, sheltered by a consensual, fraternal culture kindly emptied of any intellectual effort. Conduct resides within a perfectly well-oiled liturgy in which each person knows his ritual by heart, a requisite condition for passing to the higher grades.

This situation, therefore, avoids any confrontation of opinion. Here too it is helpful to refer back to the Masonic literature and dissertations concerning the doctrine. This is what Mackey writes in his *Encyclopedia of Freemasonry:*

A Mason is said to be "bright" who is well acquainted with the ritual, the forms of opening and closing, and the ceremonies of initiation. This expression does not, however, in its technical sense, appear to include the superior knowledge of the history and science of the Institution, and many bright Masons are, therefore, not necessarily learned Masons; and, on the contrary, some learned Masons are not well versed in the exact phraseology of the ritual. The one knowledge depends on the retentive memory, the other is derived from deep research. . . . The Mason whose acquaintance with the Institution is confined to what he learns from its esoteric ritual will have but a limited idea of its science and philosophy.[5]

He adds in his book on symbolism:

That skill which consists in repeating, with fluency and precision, the ordinary lectures, in complying with all the ceremonial requisitions of the ritual, or the giving, with sufficient accuracy, the appointed modes of recognition, pertains only to the rudiments of the Masonic science.

But there is a far nobler series of doctrines with which Freemasonry is connected, and which it has been my object, in this work, to present in some imperfect way. It is these which constitute the science and philosophy of Freemasonry, and it is these alone which will return the student who devotes himself to the task, a sevenfold reward for his labor.[6]

We should note here that the debate on the pertinence of a Masonic practice limited to the sole, unique formal exercise of a ritual learned by heart is therefore nothing new and that the matter was even then (starting from the end of the nineteenth century) prompting extremely lucid questions inside American Freemasonry itself and among its most erudite thinkers.

However, as nothing is ever perfect in this lower world, American Freemasons are not exempt or immunized from the exogenous accusations and debates that sometimes lead into more or less serious quarrels and tensions with the churches and numerous American religious communities. This occurs despite the absence of any Masonic demand for secularization—quite the contrary, as we have seen. In fact, some of these religious institutions do not view kindly here, or in the countries with a secular tradition, but for diametrically opposed reasons, the role and place of the Masonic order, which they rebuke for unfair competition by tromping through their personal flower beds.

The Masonic initiation, whether it bears the stamp of an obedience that strictly observes Andersonian Christian precepts or is secular, alarms the bulk of the clergy equally, but not for the same reasons. By very reason of the deist notion that the Order has in the United States and the difficult dialectic American Freemasonry developed in this regard, the religious community easily sees it as a second-rate copy of religion, thus an entity that could possibly begin competing with them on the terrain of spirituality. This is the case with many sects in the circle of influence of the Lutherans, Quakers, Amish, Mennonites, and the whole of the Episcopal trend. In passing, they are quick to condemn the Order's "secret" nature, which causes a chuckle when one is familiar with the entirely open exhibitionism of American Masons, who have long since broken with the tradition of discretion that is one of the foundational characteristics of the Order.

The relations between Mormons and American Freemasons illustrate in fairly exemplary fashion the ambiguous antagonism that can long prevail in certain powerful religious organizations that have built empires, like the ones of the Mormons in Salt Lake City, Utah. As Glen Cook showed in a study published in the magazine *Philalethes,* Mormons and American Freemasons have been waging a permanent power struggle since the inception of the sect.[7] The Freemasons suspect the Mormons, apparently not without good reason as we shall see, of trying to infiltrate the Order and unconfessed ambitions for power. Until 1984, the members of this sect were therefore systematically excluded from entering Freemasonry by the Grand Lodge of Utah, where the Mormons have the headquarters of their Church of Latter Day Saints in Salt Lake City. And, until 1983, the *General Handbook of Instructions* of the Mormons recommended to their adepts to "not become members of secret societies that require the swearing of an oath of allegiance."

This clearly again involves reminiscences and references implicit in the Morgan Affair even though the recommendations of Henry Clausen, a grand commander of the Supreme Council of the Southern Jurisdiction of the Ancient and Accepted Scottish Rite, led to the lifting of the ban of the Grand Lodge of Utah, and, although the restrictions no longer exist explicitly concerning Mormon desires to join a lodge, a reciprocal, profound mistrust persists.

It is, moreover, fairly juicy to note that at the beginning of the 1990s a Mormon had raised himself—but discreetly to avoid attracting any attention beforehand—to the important duties of lieutenant commander of the Supreme Council of the Southern Jurisdiction. When his ultimate ambition to become grand commander became known, his ties with the Mormons were revealed and his plan immediately checkmated. His pure and simple expulsion from the Southern Jurisdiction was the source of one of the most serious crises ever experienced by these high grades of the Ancient and Accepted Scottish Rite.

This relatively recent case reveals how the specter of a seizure of sectarian control of the jurisdiction remains present in the Masonic collective unconscious. But it also speaks of the deep and reciprocal distrust fueled by experiences that had previously scalded the two organizations. To complicate things further, the *Encyclopedia of Mormonism* still states today that the founder of the sect, Joseph Smith, had "a revelation from the Lord that the true Masonry was . . . that practiced in the Mormon temples." It is established that he had been initiated into a Masonic Lodge in Navoo, Illinois, and he seems to have drawn some elements of Mormon liturgy from this source.

On the other hand, for millions of Americans of Baptist, Methodist, Presbyterian, or Episcopalian faith, the problem of compatibility between Masonic and religious practices does not exist. This also explains how someone can be both a grand master and a minister, a situation that French Freemasons of every obedience find quite disconcerting as they are little accustomed to the customs of these Anglo-Saxon religious communities that form absolutely no part of the French spiritual environment. In any case, here the problem of compatibility between Freemasonry and religion does not even arise. It is quite simply an obvious fact.

The relationship of the Order with the Catholic Church, or vice versa, is considerably more complex. It seems fairly evident that, for Rome, semantic exercises remain without any real pertinence, and it would be perilous to seek to reserve a different treatment for Freemasons by engaging in the subtle differences that distinguish one obedience from another. This is a language that the church's flock would have trouble grasping and that would expose them to something the church is averse to revealing. It should be known that, even if the apostolic and Roman Church has considerably less weight in the United States than in continental Europe, its voice is far from being insignificant and can be heard equally well in both locations. Another factor here is the influential Irish Catholic community, which combined with that of Latin American immigrants makes a strong demographic presence.

The somewhat hasty interpretation made of the encyclical of

the Vatican II Council, *Ecclesiam Suam* (August 16, 1964), by some American exegetes and believers was tangibly corrected by the Roman authorities and their apostolic representatives in the United States. In fact, a number of Catholics initially thought they read in it that they could henceforth freely conciliate faith, dogma, and membership in a Masonic lodge without risk of excommunication or even finding themselves in a state of sin. The best-known doctrinal reaction to this subject is the extrasynodic decree delivered on March 22, 1996, by the bishop of Lincoln, Nevada, explicitly stating that membership in a Masonic order by a Catholic was incompatible with being a member of the Catholic Church and, ipso facto, *was* grounds for excommunication. This intransigent attitude had been preceded by the decrees of 1973 and 1983 of the Congregation for the Doctrine of the Faith, then headed by Monsignor Joseph Aloysius Ratzinger, the conservative German archbishop who would later be elected as Pope Benedict XVI, an office he would hold from April 19, 2005, to February 28, 2013.

The positions taken in this regard were widely publicized and spread throughout the United States, mainly through the publication on an anti-Masonic website of the "Letter of April 19, 1996 to the Bishops of the United States," signed by Cardinal Bernard Law. The problems this caused for American Freemasonry are obvious. In June 1996, the monthly journal of the Southern Jurisdiction devoted no less than five articles to reactions revealing the dismay of Catholics who had been initiated into lodges in perfectly good faith and, moreover, the desire of the Order to play for time by setting out on the path to ecumenicalism or a search for consensus.

More recently, the supreme councils of the two jurisdictions of the Ancient and Accepted Scottish Rite even jointly published a book in which they endeavored to respond to the religious detractors of the Order, in whose number were found this time—a new occurrence—Protestant clergymen who were speaking in the name of denominations that until this time had never found themselves at odds with American Freemasonry.

The fact remains that the matter was deemed important enough to compel the Supreme Council of the Southern Jurisdiction to pursue diplomacy by sending a Masonic delegation to the Holy See. It was in the spring of the year 2000 that this delegation, headed by Grand Commander Fred Kleinknecht, was received for discussions by the secretarian status of the Roman Curia with the obvious goal of defusing the situation by giving the Vatican reassurance. Nothing indicates, however, that the American Masonic high delegation received the welcome they were looking for or benefited from any meeting that was more than a simple courtesy call. It would even seem, according to reliable sources, that their Roman interlocutors—applying a casuistry that was on a par with the best efforts of the Jesuits—had invited the American emissaries to exercise their authority, claimed by the Mother Supreme Council of the World, over the anticlerical obediences (with the GODF at the forefront) before any serious dialogue could be envisioned on a hypothetical normalization of relations.

There is no need to state that the denials of the high officials of the Southern Jurisdiction did not have the slightest effect on the prelates, who, mocking them, knew perfectly well where things stood and were not at all dissatisfied with their little effort. Since that time, not only has the line adopted by Rome not evolved, but American Freemasons also have realized that this horizon remains closed.

Lastly, here is an almost anecdotal local element, but one that is of interest because of its surprising nature for Andersonian Freemasons with an ambition *to gather what has been scattered:* the Swedish Rite, which only accepts Masons of the Christian faith, has been the beneficiary since 2012 of an exemption decreed by a special commission of the Grand Lodge of New York, giving them authority to practice discrimination in the affiliations and initiations of Freemasons in accordance with exclusively Christian confessional criteria.

4

The Masonic Tradition

The Specifically American Features of Rituals and Institutions

The lodges of the first three American symbolic grades, created by different European grand lodges, also inherited Masonic rituals that these grand lodges bequeathed them. This explains why the provincial grand lodges before the American Revolution each had their own practices. After the revolution, the grand lodges even witnessed the emergence of a vast variety of rituals that had a tendency to develop in a certain state of anarchy, shaped as much by personal preferences as by the fantasies of the venerable masters. This erratic situation corresponded fairly well with the spirit of the times, with each lodge exhibiting a desire to emphasize its own identity, which was on a par with that of the civil authorities, with the lodges jealously safeguarding their autonomy against the emerging and already contested federal power.

There was a clear attempt at the Congress of Baltimore in 1843 to apply uniform standards to the rituals and restore things to order. This attempt was aborted, and a very American formulation of compromise was imposed. It was agreed that each grand lodge would define a uniform, standard ritual for its geographical area. As a minimalist arrangement this solution at least had the advantage of preserving the latitude of the grand lodges, while putting an end to that of the venerable masters, who previously had the possibility of choosing or even creating their own variations.

After the Morgan Affair, American Freemasonry experienced a new burst of popularity. This was also a period of reworking the institution. A number of American ritualists implemented works at this time that still set the rules today. It was also during this time that the first major American Masonic library, the Iowa Masonic Library and Museum, was created in Cedar Rapids, Iowa. Albert Pike, a lawyer, former Confederate general, writer, philosopher, and scholarly researcher, was one of the most remarkable authors of fundamental Masonic works. (See color plate 5 for an image of Pike.) In fact, at the request of Albert Mackey, he took part (from 1855–1861) in the handwritten revision of the rituals with a notable meticulousness. In 1859, he was elected grand commander of the Ancient and Accepted Scottish Rite of the Southern Jurisdiction and would hold this position for the remainder of his life— some thirty-two years. His most renowned esoteric and initiatory book is *Morals and Dogma,* published in 1871. The purpose of this work was to explain the symbolism of the thirty-two first degrees of the Ancient and Accepted Scottish Rite.

Pike's extensive knowledge of several living and ancient languages, including Hebrew and Aramaic, and his open-minded approach to the world made him an exceptional figure. However, as he was a figure of contrasts who had been on the side of the Confederates, who were born from the secession of the Southern states from the Union, it is necessary to qualify his humanism by placing it within the American segregationist context of his time; it would be an insult to history to depict him as a paragon of democratic virtue from the perspective of European parameters of evaluation, especially contemporary ones. Nor did he confine his activities to writing books on the Ancient and Accepted Scottish Rite; he also made notable contributions to its universal and enduring establishment as the most practiced Masonic rite in the world that suffered no interruptions.

A work like this cannot, of course, be the fruit of one lone Freemason's labors. The establishment of encyclopedic knowledge involves inventorying, analysis, and confirmation that require a wide variety of thinkers and writers. Pike had been preceded and surrounded by other renowned ritualists, such as Thomas Smith Webb, Theodore Sutton Pavin, Josiah Drummond, John Dove, John Snow, Jeremy Cross, John Barney, Charles W. Moore, Albert Mackey, and, most importantly, Moses H. Hayes, a major figure of the Ancient and Accepted Scottish Rite. Even though some of them are not so well known, each in his field and often conjointly played an essential role in the creation and establishment of a Masonic framework bearing a specifically American seal. This framework consisted of five rites: Royal Arch, Councils, Commanderies, the Ancient and Accepted Scottish Rite, and, of course, the committee system of the grand lodges, the uniform standard ritual of the first three degrees.

Today, the American symbolic lodges, thus those working with the grades of entered apprentice, fellow craft, and master Mason, are essentially heirs of the ancient York Rite and most frequently follow the American York Rite. This rite, which is derived from Royal Arch Masonry and the Templar Masonry that draws from the springs of a mythology created out of whole cloth, refers to the Templar order and its twenty-third and final grand master, Jacques de Molay. New elements were added to it in 1871—the royal and select masters.

The Initiatory Progression

The initiatory progression on the other side of the Atlantic obeys very different rules than those prevailing in Europe. In fact, in the United States, the time periods between entrance into the lodge—which is not called "initiation"—and access to the master's degree are most often several months, when they are not restricted to several weeks, the period of time necessary to learn by heart the rituals of the three symbolic grades that are passed on exclusively by oral tradition and never reproduced in extenso. As justification for this way of doing things, American Freemasons emphasize that the apprenticeship and the slow initiatory progression can take place just as easily by virtue of a practice acquired over a lifetime in the lodge. It is important to know that the activity in the lodge is actually essentially devoted to aspects related to knowledge of the tradition and the ritual for them solely, at least for those who are assiduous. That is today's big problem: American Freemasons are deserting their temples at a growing rate.

With respect to the high grades of the Ancient and Accepted Scottish Rite, which some call the side degrees (as it is well known that the first three degrees matter the most in England and in the ranks of the Grand Lodge of London), the 4th to the 32nd degrees are conferred in the span of time encompassing a weekend in the context of a group ceremony that combines the promotions, or "falls," of dozens of brother masters. This is enough time to communicate very rapidly the rudiments of these grades, which are thereby emptied of their essential content. Access to the 33rd degree, on the other hand, is much more selective and strictly reserved for a very limited number of American Freemasons.

Despite the tangibly healthy developments that have taken place since the time of the Reverend Martin Luther King Jr., the white and black Masonic communities mingle very little, if at all, in a country where, as we shall see in chapter 5, communal traditions continue to persist. The black Freemasons of Prince Hall, but also those of the more recently created lodges, such as Hiram Abiff or Omega Grand Lodges, have developed their own systems of the high grades. Although these lodges are entirely independent, their characteristics are essentially identical to those of the two white jurisdictions.

The American Masonic Administrative Structures Put into Perspective

In symmetry with American federal institutional traditions, each state, except Hawaii, has since 1813 been granted a sovereign and independent grand lodge that decrees its own rules. With respect to the recognition of third-party obediences, the Landmarks decreed by the United Grand Lodge of England, the dogmatic entity that unilaterally defines the so-called rules governing regularity, which were modified again in 1989, still provide a common platform. There are fifty of these grand lodges, which includes one for the District of Columbia, home of the federal capital. Their jurisdictional authority is exercised over some thirteen thousand white lodges, while the thirty-six Prince Hall Grand Lodges govern some five thousand black chapters, amounting to a total of around five hundred thousand black members today against less than one and a half million white Freemasons today. These are certainly very impressive figures for a European, but they offer much food for thought when compared with the more than four million members Freemasonry could claim in 1957.

In the United States, a national grand lodge would have garnered no more acceptance than an actual centralized civil authority of the Jacobinic variety; however, the United States motto, *E Pluribus Unum,* retains its full value in the Masonic domain. In fact, it is in the framework of a committee system that the fifty grand lodges manage their interlodge relations. The Conference of the Grand Masters of the Grand Lodges of North America (Mexico, United States, and Canada), which takes place every year, is equipped with an administrative office for which one of the American grand masters assumes responsibility.

It was for these meetings that the grand master of the GODF, Alain Bauer, was exceptionally invited to speak by Grand Master Tom Jackson personally and as a follow-up to an encounter co-organized by myself in Sacramento under the aegis of the relatively progressive Grand Lodge of California and its valiant secretary general, John L. Cooper III.

The event was memorable. It was the first concession-free foray of the GODF into this cenacle governed by Landmarks. The Grand Lodge of France, eternally in search of an improbable recognition by the grand lodges aligned with London, exhibited great rancor about this inroad. The GLNF, on the other hand, showed its complete indifference, knowing that the rules of exclusivity it then benefited from were immutable and were in no way endangered by this circumstantial appearance. It remains true, nevertheless, that even though it did not turn the order of the Masonic world upside down, this speech by a grand master of the GODF, in this very formal context in which major discussions are led as well as major strategic orientations decreed over which the path of consensus prevails, had wide symbolic range. All sides are in agreement on this point.

In addition to symbolic Masonry and the committee system, the American Masonic body includes four rites.

- In the Royal Arch Rite, the grade also known as mark master is only conferred on former worshipful masters of the lodges and constitutes the first of a series of five other capitulary grades. It is organized in a large general chapter whose origin dates from 1798. The local chapters are administered under the authority of a grand chapter in each of the states where they existed. This grade was conferred for the first time in the United States of America as a side degree since 1753, in the Fredericksburg Virginia Lodge.

- The Rite of the Crypt, created in 1783 in Charleston, South Carolina, refers to the sacred vault located beneath the temple of Solomon. Its origins are attributed to the wandering instructors of the time of Westward expansion.

- The Templar Knighthood of the Knights Templar, a Christian rite, was born in 1816. It is organized in a Grand General Encampment for the entire United States and has one Grand Commandery per state that administers the local commanderies.

- The Ancient and Accepted Scottish Rite is essentially one of high grades following the degree of master Mason, even though a few rare American symbolic lodges practice it in the first three degrees. It is essentially administered by two white sovereign Scottish jurisdictions and two identical black structures under the authority of Prince Hall. This system that claims a regular status governed by the Mother Supreme Council of the World cannot disguise other realities, namely the gradual emergence of more recent liberal jurisdictions in the United States that have signed the Geneva Declaration of May 7, 2005.* There will be more on this later.

---

*The Geneva Declaration was undersigned by the Supreme Councils of the Ancient and Accepted Scottish Rite gathered in an international conference in Geneva on May 7, 2005.

The oldest of the two major American jurisdictions, and also the largest in terms of membership, the geographical zone it covers, international standing, and internal political influence, is the Southern Jurisdiction (see plate 6 for its charter). Like the United Grand Lodge of England for the symbolic lodges, it asserts its universal primacy by claiming the title of Mother Supreme Council of the World. It was created on May 31, 1801, in Charleston, South Carolina, by a group of brothers who for the most part had fled there from Santa Domingo and who were commonly called the Gentlemen of Charleston.*

It was they who gave the organization the thirty-three-degree structure that is the predominant one in today's world, as it has been for two hundred years. It is also this Southern jurisdiction that administers the most widespread Masonic rite. Its administrative headquarters has been located in the federal capital since 1890. In addition to the chapters located in the Southern states, it also includes all those in the states west of the Mississippi River, with a total of some five hundred thousand members divided up among forty-two orients and 221 valleys in thirty-five states.

The Northern Jurisdiction, meanwhile, has its headquarters in Lexington, Massachusetts, and has been exercising its authority in fifteen states since 1813. These states are New York, New Jersey, Pennsylvania, Delaware, the six New England states, and, from the Midwest, Michigan, Ohio, Indiana, Illinois, and Wisconsin. Today it enjoys the allegiance of a number of adherents totaling some 350,000 high-grade Freemasons. In 1827, the two jurisdictions signed a writ of territorial distribution that sanctified these borders.

The two Masonic powers of the high grades maintain a regular and tranquil relationship. They recognize some fifty supreme councils in the world that meet every five years in an international conference.

---

*They were John Mitchell, Barend Moses Spitzer, Frederick Dalcho, Alexandre François Auguste de Grasse-Tilly, Jean-Baptiste de La Hogue, Thomas Bartholomeus Bowen, Emmanuel de La Motta, Isaac Auld, Israël de Lieven, Moses Clava Levy, and James Moultrie.

Today, and already for several years, the two jurisdictions, while maintaining their individual structures, headquarters, and sovereign grand commanders, have come closer in response to necessity and the severity of the times.

The founders of the Supreme Council of the Southern Jurisdiction have referred to several texts of the *Constitutions* to form the foundational doctrinal corpus of the rite. Those of 1762, which is not relevant, strictly speaking, to the Ancient and Accepted Scottish Rite, as it is earlier, is based on a 1758 document related to the Rite of Perfection in twenty-five degrees of the Council of the Emperors of East and West. Jean-Marie Ragon and other historian authors have cast doubt on its authenticity. The fact remains that two copies of this manuscript exist in the archives of the Southern Jurisdiction, both of which have been authenticated: one in 1797 and the other in 1798, by the signatures of Jean-Baptiste de La Hogue and by the comte Auguste de Grasse-Tilly, respectively. They were published in France in 1832 by the Recueil des Actes du Suprême Conseil de France (Collection of the Writs of the Supreme Council of France) and in the United States in 1859. Albert Pike, who was a grand commander of the Supreme Council of the Southern Jurisdiction, published an annotated edition, *The Book of the Grand Constitutions.*

The second text considered by the American fathers of Ecossisme* as authoritative, the Constitution of 1786, is attributed by some authors to Frederick II of Prussia. This document, which is deemed apocryphal today by most historians, was allegedly brought into the United States by the comte de Grasse-Tilly. With typical Anglo-Saxon pragmatism, Pike decided to dodge the question of authenticity in preference for the undeniably foundational text of the Supreme Council of Charleston. At the end of a long circumstantial argument waged with all the qualities of a talented lawyer, he concluded, "There is no evidence against

---

Ecossisme is a Masonic neologism. This generic term refers to a system of Masonic rites that was born in or derived from the tradition since the time of Chevalier Ramsay, without it being easy to give it a perfectly satisfying definition.

the genuineness of these Grand Constitutions." But he clearly refrained from asserting the opposite, and the affair was thus settled, even if the extremely extensive studies he undertook attest to the doubt that gripped him. In return for which, the debate on this subject is closed in America. It has been so without truly coming to any definitive conclusion and by emphasizing, not without reason, that we could similarly hold forth on Anderson's *Constitutions* and their origins, which trace the history of the Order back to time immemorial.

This was how, once and for all, the Constitutions of 1786 in Latin— recognized as authentic in 1834 by the Supreme Council of France— were imposed first and foremost in the United States, England, Wales, Italy, and Latin America.

Ecossisme, officially born in its jurisdictional translation in Charleston in May 1801, is in some way the culmination of a theorization going back originally to Chevalier Ramsay. In fact, it was this individual who was the first to formulate, in his 1736 speech, the idea then in vogue that viewed Freemasonry as a knightly order that was an heir to the Templars. This is how the Templar legend led, in the second half of the eighteenth century, to the development of the system of high "Scottish" grades that were heir to the English tradition of the Ancients arriving in North America via France and Jamaica. Indeed, it fell first to the Frenchman Étienne Morin to establish in Louisiana the Rite of Perfection in twenty-five degrees, terminating with the Order of the Royal Secret. Morin would later play a major role in its spread out of the Antilles.

It was his English partner of Dutch origin, Henry Franken, whom he named deputy grand inspector, that Morin entrusted, in 1767, with the introduction of Ecossisme into America. As author of important fundamental texts that form an essential source of the corpus of the Order of the Royal Secret, Franken not only achieved a work of scholarship but on December 6, 1786, he also granted patents to two Americans who would later be called on to play a decisive role: Kadosh Samuel Stringer and Moses Michael Hays. Franken also was the individual whom John Mitchell, the future grand commander of the

Supreme Council of Charleston, nominated as deputy grand inspector.

The 1793 arrival in Charleston of the comte Auguste de Grasse-Tilly would prompt a new and decisive burst of enthusiasm to the development of Ecossisme in America. Along with six brothers of the symbolic lodge La Candeur (which was created one year earlier and served as the keeper of the patents of the Order of the Royal Secret of Morin-Franken), Franken then contributed to the establishment on January 13, 1797, of the Kadosh Council and, lastly, the Sublime Grand Council of the Princes of the Royal Secret, which would be integrated into the Grand Lodge of the Moderns in 1798. Then, one year later, he left this lodge and founded, in the Orient of Charleston, the Lodge La Réunion Française, affiliated in this instance with the Symbolic Grand Lodge of Ancient York Masons, in which could already be found the names of all those who, on May 31, 1801, founded the Supreme Council of Charleston around two major players: John Mitchell and Frederick Dalcho.

Grasse-Tilly's return to France in 1804 marked the beginning of the international spread of the Scottish Rite, which returning this way to its first country became the Ancient and Accepted Scottish Rite. The rite was described by the Supreme Council of France as follows:

> Auguste de Grasse-Tilly disembarked in Bordeaux with his family on June 29, 1804. They returned to Paris in the days that followed and Grasse-Tilly, in the expectation of assignment to the army, strove to establish the new degrees within the Scottish lodges.
>
> The Supreme Council of the 33rd Degree in France was created on October 20, 1804. Auguste de Grasse-Tilly was its Sovereign Grand Commander.* The Parisian Scottish lodges (*La Parfaite Union, La Réunion des Étrangers, Les Élèves de Minerve, Le Cercle Oriental des Philadelphes, Saint-Alexandre d'Écosse*), who were in

---

*The first book of architecture (1804–1812) of the Supreme Council of the 33rd Degree was compiled under the presidency of Grasse-Tilly and is held in the library of the Southern Jurisdiction, whose staff happily supplied me with facsimiles. This historic document was the subject of an article in *Renaissance traditionelle,* no. 122, in 2000.

serious conflict with the Grand Orient of France, seized the opportunity to react. The Worshipful Masters and officials of these lodges met on October 22, 1804, in the Saint Alexander of Scotland Lodge and formed a General Grand Scottish Lodge of the Ancient and Accepted Rite. Prince Louis Bonaparte was invested with the title of Grand Master and Grasse-Tilly became his deputy. The general committee that then formed declared "that it is important that the Scottish Rite of Heredom be strictly and scrupulously retained in all the chapters, the grades of the Scottish regime being the sole know in the foreign orients and those by means of which the Freemasons of the entire world can correspond and fraternize, those of the Modern Rite not being accepted in any country."

But in a gesture of appeasement, dialogue was launched between the Scottish Grand Lodge and the GODF with an eye toward preparing a plan for union.

On November 27, 1804, Joseph Bonaparte became grand master of the GODF, and his younger brother Louis Bonaparte was made adjunct grand master. On December 2, their brother, Napoleon, was crowned as Napoleon the First, emperor of the French, by Pope Pius VII.

On December 3, the officers of the GODF and the Scottish General Grand Lodge met at the home of Marshall Kellermann, where they ratified and signed an act of union that joined the two obediences and created a new Masonic order intended to provide consistent administration of the different degrees—from the 1st to the 33rd—of the two organizations. In the following days, the Scottish General Grand Lodge (combining some dozen chapters) would naturally be led to proclaim the cessation of its activities, whereas the GODF would hold a general assembly for the purpose of examining and ratifying the shared organization plan of the Grand Orient and the lodges and chapters of the Ancient and Accepted Rite. The officials of both obediences would sign the act of union, or pact, which would "henceforth unite in one center all the guiding lights of Masonry and all the rites."

During the first months of 1805, bonds were formed between Auguste de Grasse-Tilly and Alexandre Louis de Roëttiers de Montaleau, both representatives of the grand master of the GODF. On July 21, the GODF informed its lodges of the creation of a Grand Directory of Rites, which triggered an emotional reaction within the Supreme Council, because this had not been foreseen by the pact of 1804. The Scottish Masons reacted as might be expected, and they initially envisioned—within the framework of a Grand Consistory meeting held on September 6—that there were grounds for restoring the Scottish General Grand Lodge. However, their complaints were satisfied once and for all during a September 19 meeting presided over by Kellerman, with the participation of Auguste de Grasse-Tilly and Roëttiers de Montaleau, in which the pact was modified by recognizing that "the establishment of the Directory was deemed useful," except for the following changes that were decreed.

The Grand General Directory of the rite would consist of representatives of the rites with three or five for each rite;

Each rite would form its own particular section;

All dogmatic issues or questions submitted to the Grand Orient would be passed on to the section of the rite concerned with that issue, and so forth.

Auguste de Grasse-Tilly—assigned by the marines to Strasbourg, where he should have been since November 23, 1804—actually remained in Paris. He was then assigned to Italy, where he went in 1806, and resigned his duties as sovereign grand commander of the 33rd Degree in France. He was replaced by the archchancellor of the empire, Jean-Jacques Régis of Cambacérès, future Duke of Parma and peer of France. During this time frame, Auguste de Grasse-Tilly's activity permitted the establishment of Supreme Council of the 33rd Degree of Italy in Milan, of which he was an honorary member and for which Prince Eugene de Beauharnais, Viceroy of Italy, became grand commander. The Ancient and Accepted Scottish Rite makes its first appearance in the texts of the internal reorganization of the Supreme Council of the 33rd Degree of France, drawn up on November 27, 1806.

In 1809, Auguste de Grasse-Tilly contributed to the creation in Naples of the Supreme Council of the Two Sicilies. On July 4, 1811, he took part in the creation of the Supreme Council of Spain, of which he became an honorary member. During this same time, in Paris, fourteen of the ninety-one lodges of the GODF were Scottish. On August 26, 1815, Supreme Council of the 33rd Degree of France announced through a memorandum "that it had just definitively given its blessing to the independence of Ancient and Accepted Scottish Rite by the decree it had issued in its session of the eighteenth of this month," notably specifying that the "centralization of the rites proposed by the Grand Orient of France" was not at issue.

On April 1, 1817, Auguste de Grasse-Tilly granted constitutions for the creation of the Supreme Council of the Netherlands in Brussels, which would merge on December 6, 1817, with the one established on March 16, 1817, by General Royer in the name of the Supreme Council of France. On September 3, 1818, the Supreme Council of France adopted and promulgated the General Statutes of Ancient and Accepted Scottish Rite Masonry. Several days later, on September 15, it named, on the suggestion of Auguste de Grasse-Tilly, the earl Decazes, who was a state minister and peer of France, as grand commander pro tempore.

On January 1, 1821, after two years of inactivity, at least by the Supreme Council of France, the council addressed its chapters with a circular that began as follows:

The work of the Supreme Council, long suspended due to imperious circumstances, will finally resume in strength and vigor. During this year of 1821, a veritable reorganization of the rite would be carried out, as well as on the organization of its administrative and financial levels (the earl of Valence would be named Grand Commander and the earl of Ségur Lieutenant Grand Commander). Impressive ceremonies were organized for June 24: the inauguration of the full 21-member Supreme Council, coronation of the new

Grand Commander, installation of the new officers of the Supreme Council, establishment of the lodge of the Grand Commandery, and celebration of the Feast of Saint John.

These "Scottish" round trips between France and America, which were distinguished, as is clearly visible here, by cultural idiosyncrasies and, it should be noted, political vicissitudes from both sides of the Atlantic would leave a lasting imprint on the rite. My invitation by the Southern Jurisdiction in September–October 2001 for the official celebration of the bicentennial of the Ancient and Accepted Scottish Rite, held in Charleston, South Carolina, in the fine company of the grand commander of the Supreme Council of France, Henri Baranger, and his actual participation in these commemorations clearly confirm the pragmatic realization by American Freemasons on the longstanding nature of these complex realities, as well as the Franco-American dimension, still quite evident, in the origins of these rites.

This was clearly visible at an earlier time in the writings of Albert Pike in particular. This individual believed that nothing was inevitable and there was no destiny involved in schisms and that the particular features of the rite and its Franco-American sources would allow him to get the best use out of this form of Masonic Esperanto. It was, moreover, he who in 1859 would invite the Supreme Council of the Rue Cadet to a large international Masonic gathering, although nothing came of this invitation. All this may allow those with a fairly distant understanding of these facts, or who are trying to rewrite the history, to better assess the awareness still shared today by historians and "Masonologists" of the common roots of origin. This shared legacy leaves the perspectives to be explored wide open, even if we do find ourselves confronted by sometimes divergent readings of a rite that combines metaphysics and rationality, tradition and modernity, as stated once by Yves Hivert-Messeca, active member of the Supreme Council, Grand College of the Rite Écossais Ancien et Accepté–Grand Orient of France.

American Freemasonry Expresses Itself through Social Networks

The modern phenomena of the Internet as a new form of virtual sociability and instantaneous communication in real time first began to take off in the American Masonic world in the 1990s, a good while before it gained a strong foothold in Europe. Since that time, the social networks available via the Internet have played a major role in Masonry, for both external exchanges and internal information flow, which has introduced a previously unknown dimension of public openness on display.

This observation is called for despite the fact that American Freemasonry had already been advertising itself on the roads entering towns and cities for a long time. Lodge plaques neighbored those of the Rotary, other clubs, and religious denominations without prompting a challenge from anyone. Masonic lodges formed a part of the urban landscape. Their facades are equally prominent, sporting the symbols of our Order—the square and compass—as well as the name of the lodge, often in letters of gold. Nonetheless, these lodges still remain "undercover," and it is necessary to show your credential before crossing the threshold by giving the Tyler the required words and signs in accordance with common usage but also specifying the references of the partnering regular lodge. Without these, the door will remain stubbornly closed to the visitor, even one who is an initiate. If it is a female visitor, the matter has been settled in advance; women initiates are not recognized.

On the other hand, Masonic blogs, even though they are subject to regulation by moderators, have formed new spaces that transcend these prohibitions. In addition to the fluidity they have introduced, these modes of communication have had a substantial although fragile part to play in a laudable effort to find better, reciprocal understanding. Nevertheless, the correspondence in English is still far from established on a fully satisfying pedestal, and we are undeniably witnessing the emergence of a poorly mastered bulletin board. It is a little like an upside-down triangle that raises a good many questions as the individual posts are solely the responsibility of their authors, and the obediences understandably remain quite cautious about a record over which they have no control.

The fact remains, nonetheless, that this is a radical revolution leading to self-expression and sometimes muddled conventicles that have many advantages to offer. Each grand lodge has rapidly taken possession of these new tools by developing their own websites, and the two Scottish jurisdictions, both North and South, have followed suit. Institutional moderators have been striving with uneven success to regulate these modes of communication by applying ethical rules to them in conformance with the Masonic approach. But this phenomenon, which is still in its infancy, has revealed its limits in an approach that is incompatible with exhibitionism and immediacy.

An Exceptionally Rich Architectural Heritage

An Order that simultaneously makes reference to the Great Architect of the Universe, the builders of the cathedrals, and to times immemorial from whose roots it claims to draw (through appeal to its foundations in both Solomon's Temple and the pyramids of Egypt) could hardly do otherwise, in the land of superlatives, than use the mirror of architecture to restore and physically manifest its presence in the eyes of the outside world, where it is already hardly any secret, and, why not, to suggest its power. The reference to the cathedral builders, even though it weights this appeal to the history of the Order by presuming a direct descent between the operative masons of yore and the symbolic and speculative members of Freemasonry, forms a sufficiently significant dimension in the imagination to inspire the grand lodges of the United States in their many architectural projects.

That is what basically occurred in the United States during the nineteenth and twentieth centuries by virtue of the periods of great industrial, economic, and financial prosperity. In fact, this was the time when monumental Masonic buildings appeared, displaying to American society and the world an almost insolent assertiveness that is in no way inferior to that of religious structures. Quite varied in style but always colossal and imposing, these Masonic halls stood out in urban land-scapes of many large American cities before the crash of 1929, as well as in sites chosen for a specific historical reference, as was the case for the George Washington Masonic National Memorial.

As mentioned earlier, this monument is located not far from Mount Vernon, the plantation house where George Washington made his home. It's near the small city of Alexandria, Virginia, facing the fed-eral capital of Washington, D.C., which sits on the other side of the Potomac River. The novelist Dan Brown had no hesitation about seizing on these icons—the architectural expression of a humanistic philosophy of betterment—in which he found a source of inspiration surrounded by alleged mysteries that brought joy to readers seeking escape via the imagination. The success of this literature is so well known that there is no need to dwell on it. But, outside all sensationalistic and commer-cial exploitation, a tour of the large American cities where the most emblematic large Masonic buildings were erected would not be devoid of interest, and several tour organizers quickly smelled out the makings for a profitable undertaking.

The George Washington Masonic National Memorial, said to be built on the model of the Alexandrian Lighthouse, one of the seven wonders of the world, was constructed starting in 1922. Although inau-gurated in 1923, its nine-story interior was not completed until 1970. It was dedicated, as its name indicates, to the first American president and a Mason, George Washington. It is more than three hundred feet tall and is neoclassical in style; it was built at the top of Shooters Hill. It includes several architectural elements of Greek inspiration as some of the capitals of the marble columns are of Doric style, some are Ionic, and some are Corinthian. In addition to the part of the building that has been set up as a museum, the monument houses a large auditorium and several temples. It welcomes numerous tourists throughout the year, mainly those following the patriotic pilgrimage to Mount Vernon, which in addition to being the place to which George Washington retired was also a major site in the life of the marquis de Lafayette. [When Lafayette was imprisoned during the French Revolution, he sent his son to live there with the president and Martha Washington. —*Trans.*]

The very prestigious Masonic Temple of Philadelphia, built by architect James H. Windrim in a flamboyant blend of Norman and neo-Gothic architecture, is the headquarters of the Grand Lodge of Pennsylvania. It was inaugurated in 1873 and is one of the architectural jewels of this large city on the Delaware River, which was the nation's first capital. It houses a total of seven temples that are open to visitors when they are not being used. It is not the only lodge that is claimed to be "the largest Masonic Temple in the world," but the fact is that this building, in close proximity to the city hall, is monumental and impressive, both because of its size and its style. It is also home to one of the richest Masonic museums in the world, which includes many rare objects in its collection.

The famous metropolis of the automobile, Detroit, Michigan, also claims the honor of being home to "the world's largest Masonic Temple." This imposing and extremely massive limestone construction is built in a neo-Gothic style. Its two-hundred-foot tower houses 1,037 temples and offices in its fourteen stories. It overlooks the city and resembles a cathedral but contains, in addition to many Masonic temples and the headquarters of the Sovereign College of the York Rite of the United States, no less than three theaters, the main one of which is the work of the architect George D. Mason. Public spaces, restaurants, a hotel, three ballrooms, a swimming pool, and a school confer to this complex every attribute of a large congressional center.

It is Washington, D.C.'s, pride to be home to the headquarters of the Southern Jurisdiction of the Ancient and Accepted Scottish Rite, which also claims the title of Mother Supreme Council of the World because of its seniority, just as London does for the obediences. The great temple, inaugurated on October 8, 1915, is located at 1733 16th Avenue and is called the House of the Temple (see the color insert, plate 7). It is the work of the architect John Russell Pope, who took as his inspiration the Mausoleum of Halicarnassus, which was also one of the seven wonders of the world. In addition to the departments of the jurisdiction, it contains a splendid, large temple of the Supreme Council, which is built of precious marble; several annex temples; one of the most important, if not *the* most important, Masonic libraries in the world; and a museum in its basement. It is a model for its expression of Masonic symbolism, which can be seen in all of the component elements inside and out, starting with the stone staircase flanked by two marble sphinxes.

The urban planning of the federal capital itself has been the subject of speculation concerning its own Masonic configuration. However, these allegations are due in some part to the rich imaginations of some people, and, contrary to certain assertions, no evidence exists to prove that Pierre Charles L'Enfant, the French architect and engineer chosen by George Washington to perform this task, was truly a Freemason. Additionally, the theories claiming to find a compass and square in the plans of the original city do not stand up to objective criticism. The plan is based on principles of pure geometry applied to the topography. It is certainly easy to imagine the compass therein, but it would be quite hard to find what is alleged to depict a square, because Washington and Louisiana Avenues do not intersect as they are both interrupted on either side of the Mall. This has not prevented these fantasies from feeding the illusions of some credulous Freemasons for a long time, just like the completely gratuitous speculations surrounding other symbolic images. This would be the case for the dollar bill, on which a pyramid is overlooked by a luminous delta with an eye in the center, which is supposed to represent that of the Masonic Grand Architect of the Universe.

However, it is really the Statue of Liberty that undoubtedly carries the strongest Masonic associations—and in this instance they are incontestable—in the United States and perhaps the world. The idea behind it was born following the Civil War, and it was intended to mark the centennial of the American Revolution. The project was conceived by the French sculptor and Freemason Frédéric Auguste Bartholdi during a visit to New York. Legend has it that when he arrived, he had the vision of a woman standing on a pedestal greeting the immigrants and welcoming them to a land that offered them a new life of freedom. The construction was jointly realized with the French engineer and architect Gustave Eiffel and was the result of fund drives to which French and American Freemasons made large contributions. The bronze statue, strengthened by a metal structure, is the preeminent symbol of America as a land of welcome and a beacon of freedom in the world, but it also forms evidence of the commitment of the Masonic order to continue to carry the values of the Enlightenment against the forces of darkness (see color insert, plate 14).

The color insert in this book includes photos of some of the most famous American Masonic buildings, which often offer visitors guided tours (in those cases when economic necessity and hard times have not forced them to rent out these spaces for public conferences or concerts to ensure that they have the resources necessary for the upkeep of such large properties). See plates 7 through 13.

The New Masonic Temple in Saint Louis, Missouri, was built in 1926 by the architectural partnership of Eames and Young, who took the Parthenon for their inspiration and adorned the temple with pillars topped by Ionic capitals. However, the massive corpulence of this substantial edifice is but a remote reminder of the elegance of the Acropolis. It is rather a prototype for the huge neoclassical buildings for which large American cities have an inordinate fondness. In Baltimore, Maryland, located twenty miles north of the federal capital, we also find a proud but modest temple (see color insert, plate 13) that presents a complete contrast to the imposing mass of the Masonic Temple Building in Chicago, which figures among the most conspicuous and renowned examples of Masonic architectural achievements in the United States. The Masonic buildings of Philadelphia, Indianapolis, Kansas City, and New York also appear in this photographic overview, which makes no claim to being exhaustive.

Black American
Freemasonry

In the American Masonic world, it is not surprising (except to those who are ignorant of the ins and outs of certain sociological and historical realities) to note the coexistence of two entirely separate spheres that barely intermingle: white obediences on the one hand, and black ones on the other. Wasn't it Alexis de Tocqueville who, in his book *Democracy in America,* wrote, "I see an innumerable mass of similar and equal men"?[1] One could hold forth indefinitely on this subject. He continues, ". . . who go round and round without respite in order to procure for themselves small and vulgar pleasures, with which to fill their souls. Each of them, withdrawn to the side, has virtually nothing to do with the fate of all the others." As much could be said today on the subject at hand, even though a beginning of normalized relations was launched toward the end of the twentieth century. Still today, the grand lodges of nine Southern states (Alabama, Arkansas, Florida, Georgia, Louisiana, Mississippi, South Carolina, Tennessee, and West Virginia) regard the black Prince Hall Grand Lodges as irregular, just as they do other black powers like the Grand Lodge Hiram Abiff, Grand Lodge Omega, or the Grand Lodge Saint John in Exile (in Haiti). The Gran Logia de Lengua Española of New York, whose membership consists of Cubans in exile, is tarred with the same brush.

In reality, the black American grand lodges have become long accustomed to the indifference, if not to say scorn, shown them by the white American obediences that have still not put an end to segregation and still look on black Americans as the former slaves who were once excluded by Anderson's *Constitutions*. As Cécile Révauger writes, it is hardly surprising that black American Freemasons have a somewhat abstract vision of universal brotherhood and would be tempted by a communitarian retreat within Freemasonry, given the ostracism they have suffered in the past in America.[2]

A brief reminder of the genesis of black American Freemasonry would not be out of place here. Prince Hall, a slave born in Barbados between 1735 and 1748, was emancipated in 1770, one month following the famous Boston Massacre, and initiated five years later into an Irish military lodge attached to the regiment of British General Thomas Gage at the same time as fourteen other freed slaves. He later created a lodge after having obtained a patent from the Modern Grand Lodge of England on September 29, 1784. However, the regularity of his initiation would be contested by the Grand Lodge of Massachusetts, which therefore gave no further sign of recognition to the first black lodge, which bore the distinctive title of African Lodge 1. The document can be currently found in the archives of the Supreme Council of the Northern Jurisdiction of the Ancient and Accepted Scottish Rite in Lexington, Massachusetts, with a copy in London at the Museum of the United Grand Lodge.

It was not until a year after Prince Hall's death, in 1808, that the African Grand Lodge would take the name of its founder, which it still bears today. The same year, another black lodge came into existence in another state, the First Independent Grand Lodge of Pennsylvania. The two obediences would not form a federation together until 1847, when at the same time they joined to this new body—the Grand Lodge, Ancient Free and Accepted Masons Prince Hall—all the lodges that had been previously lacking any relational structure and that had gradually come into being all over the United States, but particularly in the states of Pennsylvania and New York.

Today, this obedience is not experiencing any drop in interest and has thirty-six lodges in just as many states. It governs some five thousand black Masonic chapters that come to a total membership of some five hundred thousand brothers, as women are still not, in imitation of the regular white Masonic groups, admitted into the lodges. The three black grand lodges of Canada are also dependents of the Prince Hall Grand Lodge. Like the white grand lodges, their grand masters have implemented a committee system, and they meet once a year to coordinate their policies among each other as well as with other friendly obediences.

The ritualistic traditions of the Prince Hall symbolic lodges do not differ tangibly from those of the other American grand lodges. The same is true for the high grades administered by the two Supreme Councils of the Ancient and Accepted Scottish Rite, one for the Northern jurisdiction, established in Philadelphia in 1854, and the other, representing the South, which has had its headquarters in Washington, D.C., since 1869. The territories they cover are the same as those under the rule of the white jurisdictions.

Prince Hall also has other autonomous authorities for the whole of the side orders, such as the Knights Templar and Shriners, who take responsibility for a policy of Masonic charity comparable in all respects to that of the subordinate structure of white Freemasonry. In an American context, until the administration of former president Barack Obama the U.S. government did not provide mandatory health insurance, something that should be noted he had a great deal of trouble making the law of the land. With the new administration, the subject of health insurance and the potential repeal and replacement of the Affordable Care Act (Obamacare) is still an open question, given the state of the current U.S. government.

We have already seen that the same holds true concerning the initiation of women in America. Black American Freemasonry is equally restrictive in this domain, in which only the American obediences that are members of the international Center of Liaison and Information of

Masonic Powers Signatories of Strasbourg Appeal (CLIPSAS) are an exception.*

In the same way as female members of white Masons' families, black women are granted access to para-Masonic structures such as Eastern Star, Daughters of Isis, Daughters of the Sphinx, and the Mecca Club for the wives of Shriners; Exalted Grand Court of Lady Knights for the families of Knights of the Temple; and Heroines of Jericho for the spouses of the members of Royal Arch chapters.

Moreover, there are a number of black Masonic orders that sometimes show a tendency to claim African origins and are not at all subject to the jurisdiction of the Prince Hall obedience. Reference has already been made to several of them, but they are relatively discreet and little known. They include the International Masons, the Scottish Rite of Saint John, and the Grand Lodges of Unity, Saint Andrew, King Solomon, and Mont Sinai, as well as the Grand Lodge of the Mount of Olives. Some of these names are revelatory of the major role played by religion among black Freemasons. Connections persist, moreover, with the African Methodist Episcopal Church (AME Church), as black churches traditionally accompanied the emancipation of the slaves. Nor is it rare for black Freemasons to also be preachers, something that cannot fail to astonish a French Freemason.

However, there are a small number of black American obediences that are members of CLIPSAS. They are part, along with various liberal powers (e.g., American Federation of Human Rights, George Washington Union), of a very minor trend in the United States and maintain official relations with the GODF. This particularly concerns the Grand Lodge Omega, the Grand Lodge Saint John in Exile, and the mixed Grand Lodge Hiram Abiff, whose headquarters are all in New York. The supreme councils connected to the first two obediences cited here are signatories of the Geneva Declaration of May 7, 2005, and

---

*It was on January 21, 1961, that the grand lodges who had gathered in Strasbourg on the initiative of the GODF agreed to jointly sign the writ that brought into being this organization.

in concurrence with the liberal jurisdiction recognize themselves in the good rules respecting absolute freedom of conscience. They take part in the international gatherings of the high Scottish grades that take place every two years.

Relations between White and Black Masons

Cécile Révauger, who is unquestionably the main French specialist on black and white Masonic relations in the United States and is a university professor in Bordeaux, has written *Black Freemasonry,* an important book on this subject that includes a preface by Margaret C. Jacob. In this preface, Jacob, who is a professor at the University of California, Los Angeles, analyzes how racial segregation was established among the American brothers. Reading this book is essential for uncovering the inner workings of the very strange multicultural society of America, in which communities tolerate each other but their citizens never fraternize with one another. This observation clearly reflects the observation made by Tocqueville with which I opened this chapter.

As surprising as it may appear to a French Mason, the segregationist tradition of American civil society continues to weigh just as heavily on the Masonic edifice of this nation at the beginning of the twenty-first century. Even though the start of formal recognition is clearly present today, and we are seeing a slow thawing at the very moment that President Barack Obama's second term of office as America's first black president has come to a close, we are in the presence of a status quo. We are currently seeing a timid start of rare and exceptional reciprocal visits. This is a situation that cannot help but baffle the contemporary French observer who has been long accustomed to finding it completely natural to take a seat among brothers of all colors around the columns of the temple. American Masons of both sides today still most often prefer to heed the maxim "to each his own." The initiation of black brothers into white lodges remains the exception and not the rule.

To try to understand how Americans reached this point, it is necessary to understand that in addition to the weight of racial discrimination inherited from the days of slavery—when good and famous Masons like George Washington did not experience any qualms in this regard—the white American grand lodges have always found the recognition granted to Prince Hall by the Modern Grand Lodge of England hard to accept. It was a decision that was not without its political ulterior motives in the context of the war for American independence. The American grand lodges did not fail to view this as an intolerable encroachment on both the newborn American sovereignty and the jurisdictional territorial exclusivity on the part of the old London metropolis. This exclusivity is a principle that states that only one grand lodge can be recognized per state, and it assumed even greater importance in American eyes, as sovereignty was a concern of major proportions for the young nation.

Some enlightened Masons tried to alter this situation, first in 1899, then, more recently, after the Second World War in 1947. Both attempts were doomed to fail. The contacts established between European Masons and their Prince Hall brothers, particularly during the war years of 1939 to 1945, far from softening the positions taken by the white grand lodges, instead exacerbated their resentments and led to a hardening of the ostracism.

A more open attitude was only initiated at the end of the twentieth century and inside the United States itself, but once again it seems that it was under the effects of exogenous contacts established by the United Grand Lodge of England. Gradually, some white grand lodges have softened their positions by initiating a policy of formal recognition that has been coordinated in the framework of the Conference of the Grand Masters as well as in direct bilateral exchanges between individual grand lodges. As we saw earlier, not all the white grand lodges apply the same rules in this regard (only thirty out of fifty have recognized Prince Hall at present), and the thaw, if truly real, still remains without any noticeable effects in fraternal contacts. It will definitely take the longer time required for mind-sets to evolve, which occurs thanks to the relays of generations as well as education.

6

The Charity of an Order Challenged by Change

The Para-Masonic Organizations

Particular mention should be made of the para-Masonic movement of the Shriners. A charitable organization that was created in 1872 by thirteen Masons, the Ancient Arabic Order of Nobles of the Mystic Shrine, soon followed, in 1889, by the Gotto, then in 1902 by the Tall Cedars of Lebanon, had as its purpose, at least originally, the practice of "camaraderie and amusement." But like the National Sojourners, created in 1919 and to which membership was reserved to military personnel who had attained the grade of master, the para-Masonic orders have an essentially charitable vocation. Of these organizations, the Shriners are the best known. They traditionally recruit their members from the ranks of the Ancient and Accepted Scottish Rite who have been promoted to the 32nd degree or from among those of the Knights Templar. Today they essentially contribute to the support of social works that benefit the public at large, not necessarily individuals with Masonic connections, in an American fiscal context that is highly favorable for gifts and bequests to foundations that are recognized as serving the public good. But they were initially established as a mutual aid system for the benefit of Freemason families in a country that did not have the social safety net that had long existed in Europe.

At the head of a substantial financial and real estate empire (between 1998 and 1999, the number of centers they financed still showed strong growth, expanding from 127 to 136), the Shriners are especially known by the public at large for their exotic appearance. Most people know them from their participation in public parades, where processions of men wearing costumes and fezzes of Egyptian inspiration often ride in silly-looking miniature cars. These actions form part of a game that undeniably compels interest as well as curiosity and seems to seek a notoriety that stands in stark contrast with the discreet nature of the work of the lodge.

Let me say again that these groups' primary mission remains to make up for the absence of a public health system through their charitable works. They run a good number of retirement homes equipped with medical staffs, orphanages, medical establishments that specialize in the treatment of handicapped children, burn centers, and so forth. They will also step in when necessary to deal with situations outside the country, as I can verify through my diplomatic duties in the Organization of American States and the Pan-American Health Organization, for example, during natural disasters in Latin America and the Caribbean region. They also benefit from private donations as well as bequests but also, and this is characteristic of a very American sociability, from a large number of volunteers, as retired brothers often make themselves available to offer assistance. In just the year 1995, American para-Masonic organizations contributed upward of 750 million dollars to the philanthropic activities of the Shriners, 70 percent of which was directed to the public at large. In 1999, the Shriners organization showed an annual budget of some 300 million dollars.

The Imperial Divan is the governing body for the Shriners International. This governing body takes the place of an administration council and consists of thirteen officers. Each member of this council begins at the lowest level of the Divan and goes up one level each year, with the exception of the imperial treasurer and the imperial director.

The highest executive position in the Shriners International is that of the imperial potentate.

• The imperial potentate is both president and primary director of the Shriners International. He is elected for a one-year term.

• During the length of his tenure, the imperial potentate will visit numerous Shrine temples (assemblies), attend regional Shriner reunions, and visit the Shriners Children Hospital.

• He will perform the duties of administration council president of the Shriners Children Hospitals and of the brotherhood.

This same organizational structure can be found replicated identically in 194 temples (assemblies) in the United States, Canada, Germany, Mexico, the Philippines, Puerto Rico, and the Republic of Panama.

The Shriners organization prompted great excitement in both the grand lodges and in the Scottish jurisdictions, with whom they have long shared philosophical and structural ties, when, on the initiative of the imperial potentate, on February 22, 2000, at the Conference of the Grand Masters of North America, it was proposed that henceforth the requirement of the 32nd degree would be changed and master Masons would then be accepted into its ranks. This proposition was essentially dictated by the effects of a precipitous drop in membership of the American Masonic body and the subsequent necessity to seek elsewhere for members, for lack of another solution. The lack of members and therefore resources was threatening to make their absence cruelly felt in the short term. This initiative had the effect of a bomb. On March 27, 2000, the two grand commanders of the South and North, Fred Kleinknecht and Robert Ralston, while accepting and deploring the decline of membership numbers in American Masonic bodies, singularly those of brothers holding the 32nd degree, the traditional adherents of the Shriners, took pains, in a common declaration, to vigorously contest this approach, which they deemed unacceptable. They solemnly called for a national, unified Masonic jumpstart to reconstruct the Shriner order while warning of the discredit that opening the ranks to the master Masons would cause.

Ultimately, while the institutional ties were clearly maintained and while the posts of responsibility and management were still held by Shriners who had been initiated in Masonic lodges, membership rolls were made open to the "profane" who were more or less well off financially. The result was a certain degree of rejuvenation for this venerable organization.

The imperial potentate (as of 2015) was Michael G. Severe, a native of Erie, Colorado, who attained the rank of master Mason at the age of twenty-one, then next made his way up the ladder within the Scottish and York Rites to become a Shriner at the age of twenty-two. Today a retired company president, he had a long experience with the Shriners behind him as he began his tenth term as a member of the administration council of Shriners International and the Shriners Children Hospitals. He was elected to his top post during the annual international Shriners Convention—called the Imperial Council Session—that took place from July 4–8, 2010, in Toronto.

If, for the moment, the social safety net system patiently woven by the American Freemasons still resists the effects caused by the erosion of lodge membership numbers and therefore a reduction of results, questions need to be raised on the sustainability of their network of specialized hospitals, retirement homes, orphanages, and various social institutions. When questioned on these matters, the leaders emphasize that no correlation exists between them so long as gifts and other donations continue to flood in, in accordance with solidly established American custom. It is true that the recent opening of the Shriners is not foreign to this and that, moreover, American tax law still encourages donors to be generous for reasons that are not always cultural. Therefore, nothing indicates that there are reasons to fear the weakening of this still substantial network of Masonic charity, one of the essential elements for the respectability and notoriety of the Order and its members in the United States.

Plate 1. First American edition of the *Constitutions* by Benjamin Franklin.
© Supreme Council 33°, Southern Jurisdiction of the United States;
Lee Ewing, photographer.

Plate 2. Prince Hall and his wife.
© The Schomburg Center for
Research in Black Culture,
New York Public Library.

Plate 3. George Washington, Freemason and first president of the United States. © Supreme Council 33°, Southern Jurisdiction of the United States; Lee Ewing, photographer.

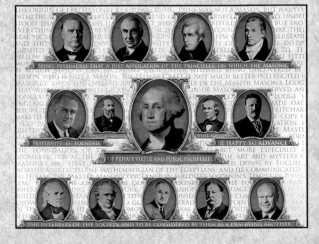

Plate 4. The fourteen Freemason American presidents. © Supreme Council 33°, Southern Jurisdiction of the United States; Lee Ewing, photographer.

Plate 5. Albert Pike, Grand Commander of the Supreme Council (Southern Jurisdiction). Portrait by Brady & Co., Washington © Supreme Council 33°, Southern Jurisdiction of the United States; Lee Ewing, photographer.

Plate 6. Grand Charter of the Supreme Council of the Southern Jurisdiction, May 24, 1801 © Supreme Council 33°, Southern Jurisdiction of the United States; Lee Ewing, photographer.

Plate 7. House of the Temple, seat of the Supreme Council of Washington, D.C. © Maxwell Mackenzie, Washington, D.C.

Plate 8. Washington, D.C., Grand Temple of the Supreme Council of the Southern Jurisdiction. © Maxwell Mackenzie, Washington, D.C.

Plate 9. Philadelphia, The Grand Temple, headquarters of the Grand Lodge of Pennsylvania. © Chancellor Robert R. Livingston Masonic Library of Grand Lodge, New York.

Plate 10. The Temple of the Ancient and Accepted Scottish Rite in Indianapolis, Indiana. © Chancellor Robert R. Livingston Masonic Library of Grand Lodge, New York.

Plate 15. New York, May 2003, Seventeenth International Meeting of the Ancient and Accepted Scottish Rite. © private collection of Alain de Keghel.

Plate 16. Alain de Keghel speaking at the Masonic Hall of Columbus, July 1999. © private collection of Alain de Keghel.

7

American Masonry Confronted by the Initiation of Women

American Freemasonry is also a family affair. Because of its prohibition on the initiation of women, a subject that is still taboo on the American side of the Atlantic, the Order has created a series of para-Masonic organizations (as mentioned in chapter 5). These organizations are grouped together in the DeMolay organization and are comparable to the junior organizations in France. For young girls there are several organizations such as the Rainbow and the Daughters of Job. The place created for women (wives, daughters, sisters, or nieces) in the movements like Eastern Star, the Order of the Amarante, and the White Sanctuary of Jerusalem is more or less akin to that of the former lodges of adoption that Albert Pike vainly strove to introduce into the United States in 1830. He personally translated the French ritual; however, it was never promulgated.

Women are therefore still absent from the American temples. This is astonishing given the influence they hold in the civil society of this great country and the combat waged by certain women to claim and win equal treatment in several prestigious clubs that until then had reserved membership exclusively for men and had continued to close their doors to the opposite sex. That the Masonic order has been spared in this battle for equality could also be interpreted that the game is not worth the candle, in connection with the loss of influence this noble and ancient institution has experienced in the United States.

The coed Masonic order, the American Federation of Human Rights, enjoys a precarious existence. The lodge brothers Louis Goaziou and Antoine Muzzarelli, both of whom were French, created the first coed lodge of this obedience in Pennsylvania at the beginning of the twentieth century, soon to be followed by another fifty-some lodges, but I am compelled to note that this endeavor has had very inconclusive results. It seems that Muzzarelli was more adept at inspiring the lighting of the fires of new chapters than at assuring their long-term survival. These co-Freemasonry lodges were most often conducted in French, which by this very fact attests to their marginal nature in an English-speaking milieu. Moreover, their claim to be a mixed Order was as far as it went. The Theosophical Society's massive entrance into the Droit Humain–American Federation (DH-AF) with the 1909 creation of a Chicago lodge that was deeply involved in this very spiritualistic circle of influence would prove to be a decisive turning point that would leave a lasting and singular imprint on this obedience in the United States.

Today the DH-AF is painfully attempting to rebuild itself after experiencing some major crises at the end of the twentieth century and showing a significant decline that threatened its very survival, in the context of an isolation that could not help but prove unfavorable to its continued existence. It has proceeded by approaching—by virtue of the support granted by the top leaders of the international DH—the scattered components of the small liberal trend of obediences that, like the George Washington Union, have enjoyed markedly greater success in a short period of time in their efforts to restore an authentic mixed Freemasonry to the American landscape. However, nothing indicates that the hour for a veritably promising albeit belated burst of energy has arrived.

The actual efforts of the Grande Loge Féminine de France (GLFF; Women's Grand Lodge of France) to try to establish itself in the United States have also not borne the hoped for results. One lodge created in

New York stopped all activity as a result of local, internal difficulties concerning operations. This obvious setback seems to have dissuaded this important female French obedience from pursuing their efforts. On the other hand, the Grande Loge Féminine de Belgique (GLFB; Women's Grand Lodge of Belgium), the little sister of the French organization from whom it got its charter, has been more fortunate in its efforts on American soil since the 1990s. It is likely also necessary to see its decision since it began these efforts to conduct activities in the majority of its lodges solely in the English language as its primary key to success; English is synonymous with receptiveness in American society. This is how it has very quickly, and with an eye toward the long term, been able to recruit a significant number of American initiates.

But, perhaps on the strength of a Belgian tradition in this regard, it has not completely forsaken bilingualism, and part of its success could reside in this. In New York, its Universalis Lodge enjoyed such stunning success that it soon expanded into the new Silence Lodge, formed on March 13, 2001, with a large contingent of initiated sisters. On the strength of this encouraging experience, the GLFB soon established itself on the West Coast, in California, with the first entirely American female lodge. This lodge bears the distinctive title of Aletheia [which means "truth" in Greek —*Trans.*] and is located in West Los Angeles. Then, with the grand lodge definitely in full flight on this side of the Atlantic, it was the turn of the nation's capital, Washington, D.C., to welcome the creation of the Emmounah Lodge, whose activities are conducted alternately in French and English.

Still in the domain of co-Freemasonry, as well as in that of Franco-American Freemasonry, a pioneering initiative was taken in 1976, in New York, with the support of the GODF on the urging of Serge Béhar, its grand master at that time. In this instance, it was an experiment to see if an American Masonic organization could recognize and adhere to the principles of secularism and full freedom of conscience laid down at the 1877 congress of the GODF. A big undertaking! Like the previous endeavors of this nature, for lack of follow-through and determined support from outside necessary for its success, the George Washington Lodge no. 1 quickly became bogged down before sinking into oblivion, although it had immediately joined CLIPSAS. The history of its somewhat laborious emergence is recounted in appendix 11, which contains a document that I wrote in 1996. Today, the success of this endeavor would appear to figure among the ranks of the most improbable wagers, although at the time that I wrote of it, in 1996, it was quite an honorable one, even though the size of this mixed micro-obedience testifies to the obvious limitations of the endeavor.

This is a worthy reminder to the gentle dreamers who persist in speculations on potential growth while maintaining chimerical illusions about these limitations. It is also of no great importance except for ensuring that the stubborn facts on the ground can be perfectly analyzed with an indispensable lucidity in the Parisian headquarters. Masonic leaders there have sometimes been a little too hasty to confuse what Americans call wishful thinking with the hard reality. While the George Washington Union, a mixed obedience, has managed in the twenty-some years since 1996 to lift itself to a level that is practically equivalent to that of the five GODF lodges in the United States, including that of L'Atlantide in New York, which celebrated its one-hundredth birthday in the year 2000, it is because in this instance it was the beneficiary of all the attentions several brothers and sisters could give it. One of these individuals deserves particular mention: Jean-Louis Petit, twice elected grand master (2000–2003, then 2006–2009), to whom we owe the immense credit of having been able to perform an unsparing audit of what separated the fiction maintained by the former grand master and founder, Harry Hendler, from the stark reality.

Based on this audit, it was possible to patiently develop and establish a culture of American obedience that conducts its activities in a rigorous and authentically American framework. Congressional assemblies are held every year that oversee the proper management of the obedience and its operations as well as the adherence of the lodges, and their brothers and sisters, to a framework that has been crafted over the course of time-tested discussions. The rituals, which have been rewritten and adapted into English, have also made the chapters the beneficiaries of a significant ritual framework. These chapters include Liberty 3, created in 1996, in Washington, D.C.; Thomas Paine of Los Angeles, in 2001; Golden Journey of San Francisco, in 2002; Benjamin Franklin of the Chicago Triangle, in 2003; and the French-speaking lodge of Raoul Zetler in Montreal, Canada, in 2002.

All the aspects of juridical, statutory, regulatory, and administrative organization also benefited from the Masonic know-how of Petit and his grasp of fraternal pedagogy, as well as from his experience as president of the Franco-American Chamber of Commerce of Chicago. These all went hand in hand with his role as a battle-hardened business leader who had created and long presided over the fortunes of a French high school in a Michigan city.

Petit's success was a gripping and flattering contrast with the improbable ventures of another Masonic brother who had tried to drag in the GODF earlier before actually succeeding, at the beginning of 2010, by promising the moon if a "Grand Orient of the U.S.A." would be given a charter! Because they utterly ignored the advice and warnings of better-informed Masons against a venture that had no future, the GODF attempted, in less time than it takes to write this, one of its worst American disappointments, which, to boot, also seriously marred the GODF's image in the United States as well as that of one of its oldest flagship lodges, the one in Washington, D.C.

This did not prevent the main author of this recent "Waterloo" from persevering in a speech that would assuredly have elicited new rebukes if by mischance it had ever been heard. Wasn't he still claiming, against all evidence, that this "assessment of a failure would only serve to conceal the great potential that exists in the USA"? This American Masonic El Dorado, for as much that it ever existed for the liberal Masonic trend that benefited from a confirmed niche, is assuredly not the one that can be found at the end of a quiet promenade or on the twisting paths toward which adventurous Masons sometimes drag

Parisian hierarchs who are barely conversant with the pitiless realities of distant shores. This is an absence of strategy that is essentially linked to the brevity of electoral mandates and the loss of collective memory they ensure, as well as to a priority granted to all that is French and closely tied to short-term electoral stakes.

The international aspects have only rarely figured among the ranks of the GODF's high priorities concerning the obediences. However, this was definitely the case in 1961 for the Strasbourg Appeal and in 1987 for the Rassemblement Maçonnique Internationale (International Masonic Congress) on the initiative of Grand Master Roger Leray. We will have an opportunity to revisit in chapter 8 this particularly sensitive aspect of Franco-American Masonic relations, which have sometimes been tumultuous, and not only for the GODF.

Whatever the case may be, whatever future might be in store for the development of an American mixed obedience, it will pass through the persevering expansion of the work undertaken by building the George Washington Union, a member of CLIPSAS. This small denomination crafted itself pragmatically and realistically by relying on the pacts signed with the GODF, while living in full independence and frankly asserting its American nature. It has a symbiotic existence with the American black obediences Omega, Hiram Abiff, and Saint John in Exile (in Haiti), as well as with the Gran Logia de Lengua Española of the Orient of New York, not to mention the bonds patiently established with the Grand Lodge of the Valley of Mexico and the Grand Lodge of Canada. The result is an original Masonic network and regional cosmopolitanism that is far from being negligible, even though the membership numbers remain modest and do not go above several hundred brothers and sisters. It is uncontestably a very promising small crucible or, as some might put it, a niche of rich potential that in this instance is quite reasonable.

A new coed American Masonic entity of the high Scottish grades emerged in the United States in May 2012 with the creation of the Supreme Council, Ancient and Accepted Scottish Rite, 33rd–George Washington Union. Its headquarters is in New York. It attests to the thus-far successful establishment of a small obedience in which the brothers and sisters aspire to an initiatory progression that goes beyond the grade of master. Its lodges of perfection were quickly established in Washington, D.C. (Sirius), Montreal (Les Pléiades), and San Francisco (Duty and Hope). They should form the foundation on which will soon be constructed sovereign chapters, an aeropagus, and lastly a consistory. A new page of history is thus being written through patient construction of a serious edifice from the ground up.

One point must be made. The question of female initiation is only at a very timorous beginning stage and remains an epiphenomenon in the United States. Para-Masonic organizations undoubtedly satisfy male American Masons but today are archaic survivals that certainly do not respond to the expectations of American women. Despite the decline of the Masonic order in the United States, and its lessened appeal as a social setting, it is inevitable that voices will be raised, perhaps in the form of a civil suit, to obtain the lifting of this discrimination and equal access for both men and women to Masonic initiation.

This initiation has always been denied to women on the grounds of Anderson's *Constitutions* of 1723. These texts, which contain "the history, obligation, regulations, etc., of this ancient and venerable brotherhood" of Freemasons, stipulate in chapter 3, "Of Lodges," "The persons admitted of a Lodge must be good and true Men, free-born, and of mature and discreet age. No Bondmen, no Women, no immoral or scandalous men, but of good Report." The question today is whether admission into a lodge is a prize sufficient to induce American women to legally demand recognition, as some did successfully some ten years ago to obtain at least a theoretically coed organization within the Rotary. The answer remains open, and it must be pointed out that the indifference of American women's organizations in this regard seems to remain total.

Does this mean there is absolutely no interest in this on the part of some of these women? Definitely not. The success of the women's lodges of the GLFF, like that of the coed arrangements practiced before the GODF became mixed gender by the George Washington

Union and the Grand Lodge Hiram Abiff, are there to confirm the real interest that exists for at least a fringe of the female component of American society. It is evident that American women today aspire to enter Masonic lodges in the same conditions as men. The rapid success of the GLFB seems to indicate a preference of American women for women's rather coed lodges. But this is only one aspect of the matter, which, taken as an absolute, does not conceal the interest women have in benefiting from the same Masonic rights as men.

Attitudes are also beginning to evolve, even if at a snail's pace, among some American Masons for whom the initiation of women would have appeared as entirely inconceivable not so long ago. As an example, look at this experience recounted by a brother in the middle of the first decade of the twenty-first century. Invited to an international symposium organized with my support in 2004 by the Grand Lodge of California in Sacramento, he came accompanied by his wife, who had been initiated into the George Washington Union in San Francisco. The presence of this sister at a conference, albeit one open to the public, inspired a huge shock among the incredulous American Masons who were confronted here for the first time by a reality that they found entirely incongruous. They were literally flabbergasted and were only able to convince themselves of her bona fides after they had "tyled" the sister.

But Anglo-Saxon pragmatism obliged that during the second such conference, organized one year later in Los Angeles by the same grand lodge, two European female obediences were invited. This time the opening speech began as naturally as possible with "Dear sisters and brothers" to welcome the sisters of the GLFF and the GLFB. Since then, the university research of Margaret C. Jacob, and more significantly the book she wrote with Janet Burke, *Les premières Franc-maçonnes au siècle des Lumières* (The First Women Freemasons of the Enlightenment Era), published in France by the University Press of Bordeaux in 2011, have incontestably helped to travel, at least intellectually, a small part of the long road—which will require great patience—toward the American grand lodges opening their doors to women.

Relations and Ruptures
with French Freemasonry

On the Close and Often Tumultuous
Franco-American Relations

The relations of French brothers with their American counterparts are easily fed on representations that do not withstand the rigorous analysis of historians. These relations are also, more often than some may suppose, the result of stakes that do not solely involve the GODF. I have discussed them earlier but will do so again with respect to the French lodges of North America. The frequent interpretations of the "ruptures" between the GODF and the American grand lodges have palpably varied and have not necessarily taken into account one primary truth: even if the system of regularity, or more specifically the rules of recognition that flow out of it, is not monolithic and authorizes a certain flexibility to these grand lodges in their relationships, it is fundamentally the rules laid down by the United Grand Lodge of England that always governs the jurisprudence of the Commission on Information for Recognition of the Grand Lodges of the United States.

Those who witnessed the great disappointment of the Grand Lodge of France in 2003, when they thought the game was won, can testify to the absolute primacy of the rules laid down by London in 1929, which have since been modified several times, the last of which was in 1989.

They are invariably applied, more or less, in the United States. And it is not the relative relaxing of these rules granted by the pro–grand master of the United Grand Lodge of England that will change much of anything in this regard. What matters first and foremost is the recognition by London, even if each American grand lodge retains a certain latitude in the application of its rules. We have seen how the sequences of the relationship between the GODF and the United Grand Lodge of England played out.

Based on a question of symbolic lodges—and as we have seen thanks to Pierre Mollier's findings—it was the failure in 1776 of a negotiation entered into in 1774 on a formal agreement of reciprocal recognition between the GODF and the United Grand Lodge of England that led the latter to send a circular telling the Grand Lodges of Ireland and Scotland to burn their bridges with GODF. It is fairly obvious that the political context of that time, mainly the aid provided by France to the American revolutionaries who had just proclaimed their independence, was not actually propitious to the establishment of a cordial understanding between obediences. The Grand Orient's refusal to recognize the primacy of the United Grand Lodge of London, a prerequisite before the official relations that had never existed could be established, did the rest. But this was of little consequence in an America then fighting for its emancipation from London.

To the contrary, in 1828, an alliance of friendship was solemnly concluded between the two Supreme Councils of the Southern and Northern Jurisdiction of the United States on the one hand and the Grand College of the Grand Orient of France on the other. The rupture with American Masonry did not come about until 1859. It was preceded, after 1832, by the tumultuous developments that were its true origin. The Supreme Council of the Northern Jurisdiction had raised a vigorous objection to the creation in New York by the F∴ Clavel—depicted as "French delegate"—of a Unified Supreme Council and of a Grand Fusion and Union of the 33rd for the Western Hemisphere. The American Scottish leadership, citing the claims of the terms of the 1828 treaty of alliance, finally reacted with a manifesto dated May 1, 1845, denouncing the activities of the GODF.

Then, in 1846, this same jurisdiction addressed a balustre to the Southern Jurisdiction, proposing an alliance "against all the enemies and attackers of our cherished institution" by rising up "against certain acts and policies of the Grand Orient of France and the Supreme Council of France" because of the encouragement they had given on several occasions to the structures proposed by Joseph Cerneau, deputy grand inspector for the northern part of the island of Cuba for the Morin Rite. What was involved this time, as can be read in the acts of the Supreme Council of the Southern Jurisdiction, was "the introduction of a rival and irregular form of Masonry of the Scottish Rite by Joseph Cerneau in New Orleans and even in Charleston, mobilizing the essential part of the Supreme Council's energy in defensive activities that alarmed potential candidates."

But some authors tell of much more precocious initiatives and recall how, in 1806, Antoine Bideaud, a member of the Supreme Council of the French Isles of the West Indies, had laid the foundations of what would become the Northern Jurisdiction, while Cerneau would form the Sovereign Grand Consistory of the Sublime Princes of the Royal Secret. The temporary consequence of these "erratic" developments was that the United States had three rival supreme councils.

The definitive rupture came in reaction to the creation of the Supreme Council of Louisiana and to quarrels dating back to 1832. It was, moreover, entirely relative, judging by the invitation extended on December 27, 1859, by Albert Pike with an eye to the creation of an international Association of the Ancient and Accepted Scottish Rite. Included among the recipients of this letter were the Grand College of the Rites, Supreme Council of France, which was established within the GODF, as well as the Supreme Council of the Sovereign Grand Inspector Generals of the 33rd Degree of the Ancient and Accepted Scottish Rite for France. The fact remains that the catalyst for the rupture was clearly present there and was gradually followed by the

American grand lodges, some of whom maintained relations until the beginning of the twentieth century, to be specific until 1913, as confirmed in the recent studies by Paul Bessel, a researcher and expert in the history of American Freemasonry who is also an officer in the Grand Lodge of Washington, D.C.

In this chapter on the sometimes-stormy relations between the American and French Masonic authorities, it is not useless to recall that this was not the exclusive privilege of the GODF. It is worth recalling how in 1995, during the international meeting of the high grade Scottish leaders recognized by the Southern Jurisdiction, Grand Commander Fred Kleinknecht and Henri Baranger, from the Supreme Council of France, had a nasty confrontation concerning jurisdictional preeminence in Romania. While the French Supreme Council emphasized its natural leadership role in the European region of the Ancient and Accepted Scottish Rite, especially in a country with a Latin tradition, the president of the American power had no intention of even conceding an inch of his new territory of influence in Eastern Europe—not even to an ally. As Baranger refused to yield to the threatening commands of the grand American brother, relations were seriously affected for a time. History also shows that Kleinknecht was not just acting in the name of his Masonic prerogatives as these were commingled with a more covert role in the service of his country. Like Ariadne's thread, we will find this constantly appearing in many circumstances and not only in France.

9

French Freemasonry in North America, Yesterday and Today

We were able to see earlier how remarkable the interactions between American and French Freemasons have been since the beginning. This is because the repeated attempts and efforts of French Freemasons to establish themselves in the United States go back a long way. But this does not imply that these relations are, strictly speaking, the result of some strategy hatched by the general staff of French Scottish jurisdictions or obediences. In the lion's share of these situations, the interactions were, in fact, the results of isolated and individual actions. They nevertheless led to a state that is worth considering, despite the fact that most of these attempts were unsuccessful.

In its conformance to the rules issued by London as well as those by the Commission on Information for Recognition by the grand lodges of America, the GLNF did not have the vocation, by definition, to create chapters on the other side of the Atlantic. When Masons of this obedience were active during their sojourns or missions abroad, they visited American lodges without any problem, preferring those that conducted their proceedings in French, like the Lodge La France in Washington, D.C. But this lodge was a dependency of a local obedience. This latitude did not exclude occasional discreet transgressions observed directly in the lodges of the GODF, which traditionally do not close their doors to visitors who are in good standing with their obedience.

Nor are the members of the GLNF given greater access than the brothers of the GODF to the solemn proceedings of the American lodges, but there are no lodges under the jurisdiction of this grand lodge in the United States. Perhaps this should be seen as one of the expressions of the American dream of the Grand Lodge of France, which, having never fully recovered from the Catholic/Masonic crises of 1964, still nurtures hopes for recognition. For the Masons of the GODF as for those of the female or coed obediences, the question simply does not arise, because the creation of chapters flowed, to a certain extent, directly from the source. If we go back to the beginning of American Freemasonry, we have already seen the decisive role played by Étienne Morin in exporting the Rite of Perfection, then of Auguste de Grasse-Tilly for the Ancient and Accepted Scottish Rite. Veritable pioneers of the Order, their companions on the journey or successors along these exploratory paths were François-Timoléon Bègue Clavel, Jean-Baptiste de La Hogue, Joseph Cerneau, and Antoine Bideaud, all cited earlier.

Less illustrious pages from the history of the French symbolic lodges in the United States also deserve recognition. It was also through them that French Masonic activities in the New World became structured. The first French lodge whose existence has been verified was created in New York by a charter dated 1760. It carried the distinctive title of L'Union Parfaite (the Perfect Union) and was essentially composed of Huguenots. It appears to have only been active for a short time. The same brothers, who had been joined in the meantime by refugees from Santo Domingo, founded the French Lodge (1780–1785) shortly thereafter. This serves as an additional confirmation of a certain diligence toward Masonic conduct to which our "brother of the two worlds" was compelled to uphold. The American phenomenon of integration and assimilation can already be seen fully at work here: the lodge henceforward carried a distinctive American name and carried out its proceedings essentially in English.

During this same period, and for the same reasons, a certain number of French Masons founded several lodges in various orients of the United States. Among them:

In New Orleans, Louisiana: La Parfaite Union, L'Étoile Polaire, and La Charité;

In Charleston, South Carolina: Saint-Jean de la Candeur and La Réunion Française;

In Savannah, Georgia: L'Espérance;

In Portsmouth, Virginia: La Sagesse;

In Baltimore, Maryland: La Vérité;

In Philadelphia, Pennsylvania: L'Aménité, whose orator brother performed on January 1, 1800, the first Masonic funeral oration in homage to Brother George Washington, who had passed on to the Eternal Orient on December 14, 1799.

Jacques Brengues has devoted a short study, in the *Annales de Bretagne et des pays de l'Ouest,* to the subject of these French lodges and their involvement in the struggle for American independence by stressing the ideological heritage shared by French and American Masons during the eighteenth century and into the beginning of the nineteenth century.[1] This Franco-American reality is duly confirmed and documented. While the majority of French lodges of this era vanished over the course of time, with the rapid integration of their French members into their adopted country, some of these lodges became part of the system of American grand lodges, obeying in this way the canons that were initially formalized in 1952 at their first conference. This is what happened with the lodge L'Étoile Polaire, which is still active in New Orleans and works in English exclusively. In New York, the lodge La Clémente Amitié Cosmopolite n° 410 was created in 1857 on the initiative of a brother then belonging to the GODF; the venerable brother Vatet always worked in French, under the aegis of the Grand Lodge of New York, which granted him the necessary dispensation. The lodge maintains a web page in French and is a member of the Committee of French Speaking Societies in New York.

It is, moreover, in New York where the genealogy of the French lodges incontestably shows, more than anywhere else in America, a practically permanent presence since 1760. Raoul Zetler was able to establish in his 1999 overview of the history of the lodge L'Atlantide, for the hundredth anniversary of this chapter of the GODF to the Orient of New York, that there were numerous initiatives that met with varied degrees of success, most often uncertain. In fact, in 1793, we had first of all the lodge La Tendre Amitié Franco-Américaine, then in 1795, L'Unité Américaine before L'Union Française, soon followed by several more lodges, one of which was an offspring of the GODF, La Clemence Amitié of Paris. Another would even be founded with the support and assistance of a French-speaking lodge of the Grand Orient of Belgium, Les Amis de Commerce et de la Persévérance in the Orient of Anvers, which would last no longer than a season.

The short existence of each of these lodges is most likely not simply explained by the fluctuating context of their era. The cultural and linguistic differences as well as the geographical distances at a time when journeys took a great deal of time are not foreign to their failure. The American integration of French and French-speaking Masons who had put down roots there sealed their fate. The difficulties induced by a gradual deterioration of relationships between obediences, the tempests generated by the quarrels around Cerneau and Bideaud, and the consecutive rupture between the GODF and the grand lodges of North America after 1859 did the rest.

In the beginning of the twentieth century, the Freemasons of the GODF seem to have finally, whether or not they liked it, accepted the need to lead a practically self-sufficient existence dictated by an American Masonic environment radically different from their own or, more exactly, that of their obedience. As we know, this obedience was profoundly influenced by social debates and by its commitment to the cause of the Republic and the great stakes in play at its founding, such as the 1905 law concerning the separation of church and state. Having experienced a close brush with disaster during the Morgan Affair, American Freemasons were deeply resistant to this and wanted no part of it. The vote of the 1877 Congress that introduced absolute freedom of conscience also made the obligation to make reference to the Grand Architect of the Universe ad libitum. This rupture with one of the fundamental precepts of the Order was regarded by American Masonry as a step that could only widen the gap separating them from their French brethren.

It was against this backdrop that the lodge of the GODF, L'Atlantide, in the Orient of New York, emerged in 1900. Its one-hundredth anniversary was celebrated with great pomp in 2000, in the presence of the grand master and an important delegation from the Council of the Order; its three younger sibling lodges in the United States also took part in the festivities. The key to this lodge's success resides in the quality of its recruitment in a relatively stable pool of one of the largest concentrations of French people and French speakers in a major American metropolis. Nor is the sociocultural substratum foreign to this success, and it ensures that this flagship lodge continues to work at an excellent level. French-speaking diplomats from the United Nations and ambassadors or high officials of international organizations rub elbows with doctors and lawyers who are members of the New York Bar Association and that of Paris, as well as chefs, businessmen, tourism professionals, diamond merchants, and a kaleidoscope of people from other professions. The stability of the brothers, who are often Franco-American, contributes to the continuity of this lodge, which stands out from its peers for its large membership.

Aware of American realities, this lodge has also bravely ventured out on the path of regular informal contacts with the Masons of the Grand Lodge of New York. In the beginning of the year 2000, they and their American brothers created an informal platform of meeting and exchange called the Band of Brothers. This original cenacle forms a notable exception that attests to the desire of regular Freemasons, on both sides, to seek out subjects about which brothers belonging to Masonic authorities that do not recognize each other can agree. Without minimizing its merits and virtues, it is necessary to bear in mind its limitations. But like the dialogue established in the Edinburgh process in Europe or in California, it is a window of opportunity, and it would be a shame to not take into consideration its ability to help break down barriers, modest as this ability might be. Just because this has arisen from the initiative taken by rank-and-file Masons takes nothing away from the qualities of this original dialogue, about which it would be delusive, however, to expect more than very hypothetical institutional rapprochements over which the players present have no control.

This chapter of the GODF long remained the only one of its kind on American soil, and we must clearly accept that its existence, like the affirmation of the principles it represents, was not always to the liking of the American obediences. There are not only the liabilities of Cerneau, which have lingered in Masonic memory, but the varied and diverse choices made on the rue Cadet [headquarters of the GODF in Paris —*Trans.*] since 1877.

It would be necessary to wait eighty-six years before another lodge of the GODF would turn on its lights in the United States, this time on the West Coast in San Francisco. The lodge Pacifica has prospered there since September 2, 1986, in a young and enterprising context that benefits from the nearby presence of Silicon Valley. Computer engineers, researchers, and young start-up creators share their life among the columns of the temple with restaurateurs and hoteliers who chose immigration so that they could take part in the American Dream. The headquarters of the Grand Lodge of California, which provides human and spiritual resources disposed to the discovery of the difference among brothers, would later encourage original explorations that would lead to meetings, after long years of dialogue, in Sacramento, San Francisco, and Los Angeles.

Then, several years later, it was Washington, D.C.'s turn. A brother, Pierre Maurice, upon his arrival to the city, made efforts to gather together several French Masons initiated by American obediences. After familiarizing them with the practices of the GODF, he won their allegiance to the creation of the lodge La Fayette 89. Its beginnings were difficult, but the first twenty years were gratifying nonetheless as the lodge was able to largely benefit over the course of time from its location in a federal capital that was home to numerous embassies and international organizations. By recruiting from these locations rather than in a disparate French-speaking milieu, it became, over the 1990s and the first decade of the twenty-first century, a productive meeting place and was often held up as an example. Like all voluntary associations, especially in areas far from home, it experienced sinusoidal evolutions at the whim of the movements of members and changes of the obedience that the brothers sometimes found difficult to manage by envisioning the developments over the long term. The professional mobility of its members—along with the preference for some to do the work quietly, protected from transient influences—would also have contributed to unfortunately reducing the standing of what was a lodge where all French-speaking Masons (who came from the Grand Lodge of France as well as the National French Grand Lodge) could rally when passing through Washington. Let's wager and hope that the virtuous circle will soon remedy all this. The creation in 2014 of a triangle lodge, L'Hermione 1780, in the Orient of Baltimore, not far from the nation's capital, seems already to be heralding a better and more promising future.

In a resolutely different context, the lodge Art et Lumière was created a year later in Los Angeles, a bustling California city and cultural center that is located two steps from Hollywood in a young population hub characterized by its openness to modernity and innovation. In addition to the usual reservoir of expatriates who have made a living in the cooking profession and settled here, we find in this lodge artists, creators, teachers, and researchers, as well as real estate agents and young CEOs who have not yielded to the challenges of a demanding expatriation. This lodge is distinctive for its youthful nature and forms a veritable Franco-American crucible. While its cohabitation with the regular American lodges remains informal, their relationship plays out more smoothly than is the case on the East Coast.

Such relationships notably authorize the shared use of temples and greatly facilitate the problems of stewardship by also encouraging individual fraternal relationships with American Masons. This is notably the case between Masons of the American lodges of Los Angeles and San Francisco and brothers belonging to the lodges Vallée de France n° 329, in the Orient of Los Angeles, and La Parfaite Union, in the Orient of San Francisco, which was founded in 1851; both of these lodges belong to the Grand Lodge of California. The obstacles to hurdle for these lodges of the Grand Orient should not be underestimated, however. The America Days of the North and the Pacific, which provided opportunities for members of both kinds of lodges to meet, have always held the purpose of helping brothers pull together to find practical solutions adapted to their environments, which often are so different from each other. To the French-speaking brothers, the American lodges were different from the remote "little France" of their lodges, and the realities on the ground at their lodges were abstract and far removed from the main priorities as seen from the Parisian epicenter, so much so that a grand master traveling through the United States could think of nothing better than to refer to these lodges with the expression "comfort lodges." These times, fortunately, now seem far behind us.

The difficulty facing the development of the lodges of the Grand Orient in the United States is moreover also expressed by relatively recent failures. For example, the triangle Mozart in Las Vegas, whose purpose was to precede the creation of a new lodge for brothers living in the famous gambling capital as well for those living in New Mexico, only lasted a short time at the end of the 1990s before sinking into oblivion.

The Supreme Council, Grand College of the Ancient and Accepted Scottish Rite also exerted its authority in this part of America, where it had accommodated the request of brothers who wanted to continue working beyond the grade of master. A sovereign chapter of L'Atlantide had definitely been created in the valley of New York following World War II. But in 1994, no lodge of perfection, aeropagus, or consistory dependent on the French Scottish jurisdiction existed in America. A network was gradually established starting in 1995, beginning with the lighting of the fire in the lodge of perfection La Clef des Deux Mondes (The Key of Two Worlds), in the Orient of New York, then that of the Lumière du Pacifique (Light of the Pacific), representing the combined Orients of San Francisco and Los Angeles, and, in Washington, D.C., the lodge bearing the distinctive title Espoir (Hope). This was followed by the creation of sovereign chapters of the Lumière du Pacifique, in the California valley, and La Triple Espérance du Potomac (Triple Hope of the Potomac), for the valley of Washington, D.C. The prospects for the creation of a North American consistory have become realistic, and it should not be long in coming.

The United States, Mexico, and Canada make up the 29th Administrative Sector of the Supreme Council, Grand College of the Ancient and Accepted Scottish Rite–Grand Orient of France. It was created in 1988 and forms the framework within which were also organized the North American Days of the Ancient and Accepted Scottish Rite, the annual meetings of all the chapters of the jurisdiction in this center with the chapters of the jurisdictions of the American lodges that have subscribed to the principles of the Geneva Declaration of May 7, 2005.

Quebec, Canada, and Its Masonic Environment at Its Beginnings

Examining the challenges posed to and by the Masonic order in North America necessarily forces us to include Canada as it takes part in regional strategies as a member of the Conference of North American Grand Lodges. But the unique situation of Quebec compels me to give it its own place for the longstanding historical, linguistic, cultural, and

Masonic ties that have endured there, as well as for the fact that its context has always been marked by a powerful Catholic influence.

Before tackling the specific case of Quebec, it will be necessary to take a short journey into the past to look at the particularly complex conditions of the establishment of Freemasonry in Canada, where there are lodges that have existed since the time of the English colony. But it is in the city of Quebec that the first lodge of Canada was formed earlier, in 1721, a lodge that carries the distinctive name of Franc-maçons Régénerés (Freemasons Reborn). It was created as an offshoot of a French lodge, Amitié et Fraternité (Friendship and Brotherhood), in the Orient of Dunkirk. In 1767, it became Les Frères du Canada (the Brothers of Canada) by passing into the jurisdiction of one of the four British grand lodges. The Antiquity Lodge no. 1 and the lodge Albion no. 2 were created in Montreal and Quebec, respectively, in 1752. Together they were responsible for the birth of the obedience from which emerged the Grand Lodge of Quebec. This was later followed by the St. John's Lodge no. 3 in Quebec, in 1788, then, in 1792, Dorchester Lodge no. 4 in Châteauguay and, in 1803, the Golden Rule Lodge no. 5 in Stanstead.

Masons were found early on among the ranks of the English army that set off to conquer Canada, where they met in military lodges. The first civil Masonic lodge was formed in June 1738, the Annapolis Royal in Nova Scotia, which received its patents from the Lodge of the Modern Masons of Boston. Charters were next given to lodges in Saint Johns (1746 and 1766), in Halifax (1750 and 1751), and in Quebec (1764). When Quebec was divided in 1791 to form Upper and Lower Canada, only four lodges remained active in Upper Canada. They were located in the Orients of Cornwall and Brockville, with the other two in Niagara. In 1788, the lodge Les Frères du Canada was transferred from Quebec to Montreal, and in 1792 it placed itself under the jurisdiction of the provincial Grand Lodge of Lower Canada.

The honorable Claude Dénéchau, who signed the charter forming the regular lodge Les Frères du Canada, was the first Canadian to be named grand master of a grand lodge in Canada. This was followed by the creation of lodges in the new provinces: in British Columbia (1859), in Manitoba (1864 and 1870), in Alberta (1882), and in Saskatchewan (1883).

In 1855, thirty lodges of western Canada and Quebec combined to form the Grand Lodge of Canada, and the old Masonic lodges formed their own grand lodge two years later. In 1869, Quebec formed its own grand lodge. The Grand Lodge of Canada, located in Ontario, refused to recognize the autonomy of Quebec, a decision supported by the Grand Lodge of England. However, the Masons of Quebec received the support of the more important Grand Lodges of the United States, and it was the grand masters of the Grand Lodges of Vermont and Maine, who had already recognized the Grand Lodge of Quebec, who assisted at the installation of the grand master of this grand lodge. A short time later, at its congress of July 8–9, 1874, the Grand Lodge of Canada recognized the autonomy of the Grand Lodge of Quebec.

What we see in draft here is a Masonic North American landscape that also explains the inclusion of the Canadian grand lodges in the Conference of the Grand Masters of North America. It can be seen in passing that London had been compelled to follow an initiative taken by the American obediences, whereas the United Grand Lodge of England still refused to take into account certain geopolitical developments. In 1887, the Grand Lodge of Canada changed its name to reflect the provincial nature of Canadian Freemasonry: it would henceforth be known as the Grand Lodge of Ancient and Accepted Masons of Canada in the Province of Ontario.

The difficulties encountered by Freemasonry, which was prey to the hostility of the Catholic clergy, were not slow to make their presence felt in Canada, where, in 1771, the superior of the Sulpicians and the lord of Montreal, Étienne Montgolfier, attacked the Order. This was followed, in 1794, by the incrimination of the Order by the lieutenant-governor of Upper Canada, John Graves Simcoe, who feared an insurrection fomented by the Freemasons of Montreal, whose close relationship with those of the neighboring state of Vermont were deemed suspicious.

The antagonism between Canadian Freemasons and the Catholic Church left a lasting imprint on the country's strained relationship with the Order and its place in this country. This was not merely on the basis of Masonic liberal activism since 1896 and the creation that same year of the lodge L'Émancipation, a driving force for secularism and a crucible in which simmered the debate over church and state relations and mandatory education. This is what compelled Henri Bernard to claim that two perils threatened the intellectual life of Montreal at the beginning of the twentieth century: one Anglo-Protestant and the other Masonic.

There was a significant group of French-speaking Masons at this time in Montreal, several of whom had been initiated in France. It was in February 1909 that the turn of events became more complicated with the expressed ambition of the Catholic Association of French-Canadian Youth to purge Montreal public life of all Masonic influence. This was how several of its organizers became involved in fantastic events intended to destabilize the Freemasons of this extremely Catholic province. Leading members of this association rented a spot located above the studio where the lodge L'Émancipation met so they could eavesdrop. The Catholic mayor, an Irish native, M. Guérinn, who was a close associate of Monsignor Bruchési, requested that an investigation be launched of the lodge, which he accused of entertaining vague plans for disrupting the Eucharistic Congress of 1910. But the legal authorities refused to press charges. However, just as another trial had ended with the acquittal of all the incriminated Masons, the Catholic Association of French-Canadian Youth gained possession of a list of the lodge members and made it public, the immediate effects of which were the loss of their employment by many Masons, the banning of the organization, and the dissolution of the lodge.

These episodes vouch for the power the Catholic clergy had long wielded to discourage Quebecers from joining Freemasonry, whose initiates—according to the church—were hatching dark plots against religion and the state. During this time the Catholic clergy enjoyed considerable influence in Quebec, with its largely illiterate populace that had been weakened by its cultural and linguistic isolation. But the Freemasons refused to give in to resignation, and a new lodge with the name Force et Courage was founded on March 16, 1910, and remained active into the middle of the 1940s.

This context should not conceal another reality that concerns the confirmed or presumed membership in the Order of important Canadian figures. This group includes several former Canadian prime ministers or ministers and a number of other politicians and civic notables, at the forefront of which we find Joseph-François Perrault (1753–1844), considered the father of education in Canada; Laurent-Michel Vacher, a philosopher and writer from Quebec; J. Z. Léon Patenaude, founder of the League of Rights and Liberties; and Peter McGill and John Molson, two former presidents of the Bank of Montreal. William Badgley, a judge and the former attorney general of Quebec, was even a grand master.

Our North American French-speaking Masonic panorama would contain a significant gap if we neglected to examine Quebec's Canadian lodges in greater detail by not recalling the first steps taken by the Order in this vast land. The problem is complex, and, to truly answer it, we would need to provide a more detailed study than can really be addressed in the context of this book, which seeks to furnish a general overview. Let us simply recall the particular context of la Belle Province: the weight of an old and well-established Catholic tradition that was hardly favorable to the establishment of Masonic lodges. In addition to this are a strong identity awareness that never forgets its ancient ties, which are not only linguistic but also stem from Breton emigration, the painful pages of history, and the famous visit of General Charles de Gaulle in 1967 and his vibrant cry of "Long live Free Quebec!" Direct, sincere, close, privileged—there is no lack of adjectives for describing the nature of the relationship between France and Quebec. It has left an equal imprint on the context in which Freemasonry evolves, which does not escape the phenomena of mimicry or those of the Montreal microcosm into which the expatriate French have integrated.

Three French-speaking lodges of the Grand Lodge of Quebec deserve mention here: the lodge Les Coeurs Réunis n° 45 (Hearts Reunited), founded in 1870; the lodge Dénécheau n° 80, founded in 1906; and La Renaissance n° 119, whose fire was lit in 1947. All three are located in Montreal.

Next to the United Grand Lodge of Quebec, whose influence and means are far from negligible, there are a fairly large number of chapters belonging to obediences of average or small numerical significance. Note the unusual degree of fragmentation within an already limited and complex recruiting pool, which likely does not facilitate the reading or harmonious development of liberal lodges and obediences; those that prevail on the recognition from the United Grand Lodge of England are predominant. In addition to the weight of history, those of liberal sensibility that are unrecognized by London are placed in a competitive situation. Of these we find a lodge that is a dependency of the Grand Lodge of France, which survives as best it can, and for about twenty years, a mixed obedience—Le Droit Humain of the Canada Federation—which fares somewhat better and has a presence on the Internet.

The National Grand Lodge of Canada has undertaken the task of gathering together these scattered pieces and has gradually integrated lodges like Champlain and Phoenix. The Universal Grand Lodge of Quebec consists of two lodges, Melchisédech and Pentagramme, both coed and working in the Ancient and Accepted Scottish Rite. The North American obedience George Washington Union has also established a mixed lodge there, Raoul Zetler, which seems to have found its footing and forms a pole of stability protected from the turbulence that regularly rattles the Masonic microcosm of Montreal. Following a Grand Orient of Canada in 1992, a Grand Orient of Quebec appeared in 2012, which has one single lodge, Les Amis Réunis. A National Grand Orient of Canada emerged in turn in 2013 with the creation of a lodge named Émancipation, a successor to Montcalm Nouveau Monde, the result of an earlier split of the local lodge from the GODF, whose title had been Grand Orient de Canada. With its only Quebec lodge created in 1999 under the distinctive name of Force et Courage, the GODF encountered recurring difficulties that are partially similar to those that the Grand Lodge of France experienced with its lodge, with the brothers forced to overcome mainly financial obstacles to meet their responsibilities. The survival of the GODF lodge remains fragile. It was already the successor of the Maillon Laurentien, which was dissolved a short time earlier after two other chapters had suffered the same fate.

The Jurisdiction of the High Grades of the Ancient and Accepted Scottish Rite in Quebec

With respect to the high grade structures in Canada, it was not until 1845 that the Northern Jurisdiction delivered its grand charter to the Supreme Council of England and the country of Wales, which in turn in 1874 created the Supreme Council of Canada. This council exercised authority over the structures of the rite, which had preceded it since 1838 in Hamilton and London in Ontario; St. John, New Brunswick, in 1868; Halifax, Nova Scotia, in 1870; and Toronto and Montreal in 1873. However, similar to what we know of its position in Great Britain, the Ancient and Accepted Scottish Rite remained a Scottish authority of relatively modest importance in a Canadian environment dominated by the tradition of the Ancients—which is to say the Emulation Rite— as well as the York rites and those of the Royal Arch.

The complexity of the liberal Masonic landscape in Quebec is again visible in the high grades, even if it is less so in the symbolic lodges. The ephemeral French-speaking Supreme Council of Canada, created with a grand charter from the Supreme Council of France, maintained relations with the Scottish authority of the GODF that was the Grand College of Rites until 1999. Following its collapse in 2000, a new juris-diction appeared that had received its grand charter from the Supreme Council, Grand College of the Ancient and Accepted Scottish Rite–

Grand Orient of France. It signed the Geneva Declaration of May 7, 2005, and has been entered, in the capacity of an observer, in the international meetings of the Scottish high grades.

From its merger in December 2013 with the Supreme Council of the Universal Grand Lodge of Quebec has resulted the new Unified Supreme Council of Canada, which, at the end of a process nearing completion, will exercise jurisdiction over four lodges of perfection, three sovereign chapters, three philosophical councils, and a consistory numbering a few more than one hundred brothers and/or sisters. Also in relationship with the Supreme Council for the Ancient and Accepted Scottish Rite 33rd Degree—George Washington Union and its perfection lodge in Montreal, Les Pléiades, the two authorities apply rules of interlodge visits and dual affiliations. As a result, they should form a pole of stability, the center of the Union of the Ancient and Accepted Scottish Rite, propitious for a harmonious development and offering all of its members, both men and women, their preferred path into unity and fraternal concord.

The universe of Quebec, and most particularly Montreal, which is both English- and French-speaking, is formed from a convergence of paradigms in which the Ancient and Accepted Scottish Rite proves again to be the most apt at fulfilling its universal mission and serving what many have gladly labeled, not without reason, Masonic Esperanto.

A Little American
Masonic Perspective
in a Changing World

In a world of large populations and rapid changes that cause shifts in the traditional gravity centers, Anglo-Saxon pragmatism could truly have some surprises in store, which the pro–grand master of the United Grand Lodge of England, Spencer Douglas David Compton, Lord Northampton, has been toiling with in London. Some portentous echoes of possible movements in North America, like elsewhere in the world, are visible.

Translated into geostrategic concerns, these echoes could not help but have a considerable impact, first and foremost in the sphere of the most direct American influence as defined by the Monroe Doctrine. This U.S. governmental policy extended to the whole of Latin America and the Caribbean, two powerfully vital pools of Masonry, of which Cuba is no minor part despite the political opinions of the Castro regime. It is common knowledge that the relations between Cuban Masons and their American brethren have endured despite the embargo imposed by the United States. All this with the permission of Fidel Castro.

It is also by including all the background information in the potential arguments that we are best able to measure the full extent of the initiatives taken by the leaders of the United Grand Lodge of England since 2007, by means of a new kind of conventicle under the cover of study and research in Edinburgh. These efforts are worth lingering over for a moment, especially because in 2011, American Masons hastened to follow suit by organizing a similar exercise in Alexandria, Virginia. It is common knowledge that from the beginning this has involved conducting informal reflections in a research context to begin to imagine the contours of a Masonic universe that will not long escape the important changes experienced by our global village.

Because the Grand Lodges of Scotland and Ireland are stakeholders and associated with these impartial and unprecedented meetings between researchers who are officially devoted to a purely scientific approach, the more diligent American obediences have not been late in taking an interest in them as well. They saw there a window of opportunity to seize, thereby confirming again their immutable ability to enter a new dynamic of the Order. The opposite would have come as a surprise to all those who know this country of pioneers who always remain alert and ready to seize the opportunity to face new challenges. Jean-Jacques Servan-Schreiber, an astute expert on the United States if ever there was one, was the "awakener of the shadow," one of the first to alert the French public about this with his famous book *Le défi américain* (The American Challenge). (The original French title of my book, *Le défi Maçonnerie américain,* echoes his title.)

In fact, the equation is fairly simple: the Order will certainly be celebrating its tricentennial in 2017, but it is seriously threatened in the very heart of the land that served as its cradle. Its membership numbers have dropped dangerously. Its decline has been swift, and the United Grand Lodge of England no longer has more than 230,000 Masons, the median age of whom is high, moreover. (This amounts to a loss of some 140,000 members in ten years.) There has been a dramatic drop in younger members, and the number of lodges is rapidly shrinking. There are no longer more than eight thousand. The institutional uncoupling has been equally obvious since Tony Blair, when he was UK prime minister, adopted a hostile stance toward the United Grand Lodge of England. (His wife and children were Catholic, and he converted after leaving office.) Thus was undone definitively the trinity of throne-church-Masonry. Henceforth, the moment for pragmatism appears to have come, and the English have always shown the ability to be practical when it counts.

It was incontestably a consequence of this that the idea was launched in 2007 to engage in a new kind of dialogue, without too many preconditions, by momentarily putting the Landmarks to the side, and to sit around a table to engage in brainstorming peacefully and constructively, this time on the level of official representatives who wish to share a purely cerebral kind of thinking. The delegates of the three allied grand lodges (United Grand Lodge of England, Grand Lodge of Ireland, and Grand Lodge of Scotland) then presented the idea of classifying the different orders of Masonry into five main categories, the first three of which are

The recognized regulars, because, to make things simple, regularity is not enough on its own for recognition;

The unrecognized regulars;

Then, in a display of unprecedented boldness, in the third position would be the grand lodges for women, which obey the rules of regularity except for the truism that they initiate women, which obviously contravenes a Landmark.

This is likely the most significant new sign of the evolution of the mind-sets and the pragmatic realism of the British, soon shared by those in the United States, as the 2014 conference of the grand lodges in Baltimore can confirm. In fact, for the rest, the two other categories of historical continental irregular obediences are certainly mentioned in the catalog, but with no illusory expectations on either side for any doctrinal advances, and thus intervisits are not part of the agenda. These other categories of obediences, placed last, evidently overlay most particularly the ones that are mixed and thus seem today definitely too far removed from the regular galaxy to foster any hopes of institutional reconciliation in the foreseeable future. (When coupled with the developments that have taken place at the GODF since 2010 on the coed question, these conclusions speak for themselves.) But the fact remains that a signal for movement has been given, and this is what history tomorrow will retain, whatever the results of this kind of approach may be. The sliders are therefore moving.

The stakes can be summed up in a simple equation: advance by means of an international dialogue a framework in which Freemasons can still bring much to the table, on the condition that they truly break the cycle of eternal dogmatic and doctrinaire intolerance that does not spare institutions. But other experimental paths are being explored pragmatically. If this should lead to some still rather improbable consensus, the result would be a Masonic perestroika. Without being totally beatific, let's place a modest wager, without excessive illusions or precautions, on the windows of opportunity that have been partially opened this way under the pressure of increasingly well-founded realities.

Realization of the existential peril could explain a new type of approach, for want of anything revolutionary. Who could have imagined for even a moment that obediences that had always been considered irregular, according to the canons of the Landmarks, would be included in a strategy initiated by London? However, we can see the serious nature of lodge work there, which, when stamped "historical," is considered in a perspective that is quite far from any regularization of relations. It is important to neither underestimate nor remain ignorant of these tectonic plate movements and to not nurture vain hopes by way of renunciations that the weight of history excludes.

Distrust and resistance have not been slow in putting in an appearance. Their first consequence was the replacement in 2009 of the English pro–grand master Lord Northampton, who wielded authority in a practical manner but who was evidently deemed too innovative by a dyed-in-the-wool conservative faction. Another consequence was the withdrawal of the United Grand Lodge of England, which financed the Centre for Research into Freemasonry at the University of Sheffield, which was headed by the Swede Andreas Önnerfors, who was overly receptive, in the opinion of the conservatives, to the uninhibited academic overtures that until that time had been supported and subsidized by the executive branch of the obedience. The inevitable result was the closing of the center, and we can clearly see here the limits of the influence of the reform elements that are still toiling to establish themselves, while the flagship is still trying to determine its course or even taking on water.

And if America were to pick up the baton? Already the topic of discussion for the Conference of North American Grand Masters includes some revealing clues of their thoughts on refocusing the Masonic debate around values: how to restore a sense of citizenship, become a moral compass, and stress the difference. Even if the grand lodges listened without coming to any conclusions, it appears that a space of discussion and reflection was opened, which marks a rupture with the usual monotony.

It is also important to note that Masonic works of scholarship have rarely shown such great variety and richness, which until recently has not been the case in the various contexts of the research lodges on both sides of the Atlantic. However, for years now the Research Society of the Southern Jurisdiction has welcomed researchers of whom it demands no conformance with any criteria of regularity and makes no conditions concerning recognitions. The only thing that matters is their qualification.

The various research centers have the Quatuor Coronati Lodge in London for a model. And even if this "authentic school" of Masonic research has lost a little of its luster, its rigorous scientific method has earned it disciples in both the Old and New Worlds. The work performed there remains noteworthy. The centers offer a surprising contrast between the dominant obediential dogmatism and the high degree of scientific standards of the researchers, who work with a great mental freedom. These cenacles, with whom are sometimes pragmatically integrated Masons who do not heed the canons of the Landmarks, work free of the searchlights that, like funhouse mirrors, maintain futile illusions of power. These protected spaces are also often laboratories of ideas and the ideal sites for top-rate encounters without any preconditions. They are possible experimental crucibles for exploring the future and imagining a foreseeable Copernican transformation of the United Grand Lodge of England, with the consequences and repercussions that this would bring about in North America. We have not reached this point yet, but the tricentennial of the Order is upon us and can still hold some surprises.

For the time being, we should not lose sight of the resistance noted earlier that testifies to the difficulty involved in moving forward on the path of the center of union that the founders of the Order had in mind, as noted in Anderson's *Constitutions* of 1723. A very recent warning was issued by the representative of the United Grand Lodge of England at the closing of the October 2013 session of the lodge Quatuor Coronati against "undesirable effects that certain positions could have on regularity and unity," which was noted during the session of the Bayreuth research lodge and was immediately passed along by the Senate of the United Grand Lodges of Germany and the grand masters of the German obediences. However, this served merely to remind members of the eminently humanist and nonreligious vocation of the Masonic order, but it was sufficient to inflame the debate between the supporters of a continental European tradition and the unconditional deists.

In the final analysis, and by placing the challenges of the moment within a global context, including the United States, despite a small note of modest optimism, the destiny of the United Grand Lodge of England remains more uncertain than ever. This is a dimension that cannot be concealed when the question of analyzing the major stakes is raised. The consequences of its almost unavoidable weakening cannot fail to have worldwide repercussions because of its historical significance and the powerful Masonic networks founded upon it—in a mechanism that has been perfectly mastered until the present.

What could these consequences be? What role could American Masonry, which is also weakened but still quite powerful and in possession of resources we should not underestimate, and which shares fairly similar interests, play in filling the vacuum? Will the pragmatic and conscious elements of those tackling the major risks allow them the time they need to overcome the final pitfalls? And what could the effects be on the obediences connected to the United Grand Lodge of England and on our own liberal networks? These would be our questions.

We can already see the emergence of these major stakes at the large meetings, like that of the Conference of the Grand Masters, where an evolution could be sensed. But it will still be necessary to engage in a substantial study of prospective changes that remains to be undertaken by the forecasters, by placing at the epicenter, henceforth and with a new realism, no longer London but the American grand lodges. Between a congealed tradition and a decline, there is most certainly a reformist middle ground on which there is still time for Masons of goodwill and all sensibilities to labor, mindful only of the center of union, which is to say without anyone being unreasonably constrained.

Is the Overall Decline in Membership the Herald of Profound Changes?

An update is called for at the end of this quick scan of the history and singular features of the Masonic order in America: Freemasonry of the United States has recorded a significant decline over the past several decades. This is an implacable reality, even if the rate of this shrinkage is currently experiencing a slowdown. At the end of the Second World War, we saw a tangible increase in membership, which reached a height of four million Masons in 1957. In 1964, the arrow on the chart began pointing downward at an annual rate of 3 percent, and by the year 2000, membership was already no more than two million.

These figures are smoothed over and cover realities that vary from one state to the next. California, the fourth largest Masonic reservoir after Pennsylvania, Ohio, and Texas, has lost 42 percent of its brothers between 1998 and 2010, while the grand lodge of the state of New York has recorded a decline of 34 percent, and that of Montana is only 5 percent.

The total number on December 31, 2013, was estimated to be 1,300,000. Out of the entire population of the United States, the average ratio remains 0.4 percent, which is comparable to that of European countries, which in the best of cases never goes higher than 0.25 percent. Nobody will contest the significant decline in the number of American Masons. But what some are quick to label a "descent into hell" is worth putting into perspective and can be explained by several parameters.

The first parameter is of an almost universal order and touches on a social phenomenon that has produced a general estrangement that affects group activity within a context of many competing demands of all kinds. In American society, where the individual tends to be judged, with a strong dose of pragmatism, on his or her achievements and work performance, the place made for philosophical commitments has been necessarily reduced. Furthermore, the original social function of American Freemasonry, which has long made up for the deficiencies of the government in regard to social, sanitary, medical, and educational matters, has recently been assisted, in some aspects, as the result of protective legislations enacted by the Obama administration. Certain traditional niches of activity occupied by the American brothers and their lodges have been fortunately taken over by arrangements modeled on the social safety net that Europeans have long enjoyed.

But these arguments cannot fully explain everything. After a prolonged analysis of Freemasonry's evolution, reflecting on what distinguishes and sometimes opposes French and American Masonry, with their two fundamentally different notions of the Order, it is clear, with no arrogance intended, that French Freemasonry in all its elements, as opposed to its trans-Atlantic counterpart, continues to inspire an unfailing interest among people, including the young, who are flocking toward the lodges of the different obediences. Of course, the strong constraints imposed by daily life, as well as the impact of greater equality between the sexes, lead the profane to knock on the door of the temples a little later than was the case a few decades past, but the flood remains and, this is undeniably more important, the diligence as well.

This now consistent numerical erosion of the Masonic entity in the United States, while it seems to delight certain denigrators given to analyses lacking all subtlety, cannot nor should not be a matter of indifference to Masons elsewhere. In fact, everything that saps the strength on any one Masonic entity is harming the whole of Freemasonry on a universal scale. So it is no longer a question of taking satisfaction in a display of *Schadenfreude* and thinking that the space thus freed could simply be occupied by those who have a more progressive vision of the Order. This is a notion that is, moreover, quite bizarre—one that no one could confuse with the progressive nature of the initiatory process and which could provide the subject of more extensive considerations already studied elsewhere, as the confusion of the terms could lead straight into veritable misunderstandings and not only semantic ones.

The Demographic Pressure of Immigration and the Difficulty in Predicting Its Effects

Since the arrival of the first European colonialists in the sixteenth century, more than fifty million immigrants have settled in the United States. Until 1940, the vast majority of immigrants came from Europe. Their numbers were small until the 1830s, but they began arriving in more massive numbers from 1840 to 1850, initially the British and Irish. Immigration expanded in the final quarter of the nineteenth century to include people from the countries of Mediterranean Europe (especially Italy) and Central Europe (often the Slavic countries). More than twenty-three million immigrants flocked to America between 1880 and 1920.

Starting in the 1920s, the United States, wishing to put the brakes on immigration, established a system of quotas. The economic crisis of the 1930s only reinforced this tendency. A new form of immigration developed after the Second World War. These immigrants were mainly political refugees from Eastern Europe, anti-Castro Cubans after 1960, and Southeast Asians (Vietnamese, Cambodians, and Laotians) after 1974.

Today, immigrants essentially come from third world countries:

Latin America (primarily Mexico) and Asia (Korea, the Philippines, Vietnam, and so forth). In the 1990s, a new migratory current appeared that came from the former Communist nations in Europe. Moreover, illegal immigration has probably become larger than legal immigration. This, by definition, remains difficult to quantify, and the numbers are based on questionable extrapolations. It is commonly accepted that this has increased since the 1990s because of the economic downturn that affected Latin America, because more than half of the clandestine immigrants come from Mexico.

In a country that establishes statistical differences that the European nations condemn, more than thirty-four million black Americans were recorded in the 2000 census. Latino minorities now represent more than thirty-eight million people in the United States. A name distinction is established based on the native region or country. *Hispanics* is the generic term for those who speak Spanish, while to designate Americans of Mexican origin specifically, the term *Chicanos* is sometimes used. During the closing decade of the twentieth century, the Hispanic majority grew by 58 percent while overall demographic growth was only at the rate of 13.4 percent.

Hispanics have therefore become the largest minority group in the country, slightly larger than the black community. They are concentrated in the western and southern United States, with half of this number in Texas and California, but their communities are growing visibly larger in the states of Illinois, New York, and New Jersey. Mexicans (or Chicanos) form the largest group (58 percent), but their proportion is shrinking as more immigrants arrive from the rest of Latin America, including South America and the Caribbean.

Regarding the white majority, Latinos have chosen to define themselves as a nonwhite minority. Asian immigrants, whose number was no more than 1.5 million in 1960, are now at five million, with the Vietnamese and Cambodian communities representing the lion's share of that increase. Asian immigrants tend to cluster on the West Coast. For example, more that 70 percent of Japanese immigrants live in California and Hawaii, while more than half of the Chinese live in California and New York.

The most recent demographic projections forecast there will be a total of 420 million inhabitants of the United States in 2050. This population would include close to 105 million Latin Americans, 60 million African Americans, and 35 million Asian Americans. In less than fifty years, the American white demographic will thus be reduced to only 53 percent of the total United States population. And from 2050 to 2090, their part of the population is projected to shrink to less than 30 percent.

The keepers of a society that has been traditionally based on the WASPs (white Anglo-Saxon Protestants) have good grounds to question their prospects in a changing melting pot. The American sociologist Herman Sullivan has already sought to replace this notion with five categories arising from American immigration: he establishes a distinction between assimilation, acculturation, domination, a cultural two-party system, and segregationist rejection. The limits of this book do not allow me to venture further into this approach, but it is interesting in more than one respect, as it is the reflection of the real America and projects us toward that of tomorrow. It is easy to see the serious challenge that will confront Freemasonry in the profound upheaval of a society that will then be constrained to build with totally exogenous and polymorphous contributions and will be forced to face the rising power of the religious sects that are brought in and spread by Latino immigrants. These sects have often been given new life by their importation into a Latin America that has lost interest in traditional Catholicism. The American spiritual constant finds here a new dynamic whose possible effect on Freemasonry, however, remains difficult to gauge in this large country in perpetual motion.

On another level, but one that is not entirely neutral, it has already become difficult today to claim that the United States is still a monolingual nation given the fast progression of Spanish that, despite its uneven progress depending on the state, has allowed it to pose a significant challenge to the monopoly of the English tongue. Even if right now there is nothing dire in a correlation between these changing American demographics and their various consequences, as projected today by the sociologists and forecasters, we are not seeing members of these new groups—which could have been a source of regeneration for Freemasonry—flocking to the lodges. Therefore we can't foresee that they will have enough of an impact to make a difference on American Freemasonry. What we see here is a challenge that is entirely specific to the United States, which is paying the price of a fascination with the American dream on the part of many people in a good part of the planet, first and foremost the often disinherited populations living in the intra-American continental environment and, to a lesser degree, the Pacific.

Because of these changes in demographic perspectives and the effects they are causing, and the more extreme effects they will cause tomorrow, it is important to consider the evolution of American Freemasonry, and not merely in quantitative terms. What will be the consequences of the expected influx, which is already forming a heavy burden? Will the American Masonic order be able to prove itself up to the task of integration, which is one of the constants of this nation? Or, to the contrary, will the forecasts of Herman Sullivan of an increased partitioning of America find a counterpart in American Masonry, whose numbers are far from being the largest in the world?

Already in this last regard, it is important to put the numbers into context and compare them by drawing in several parameters that will permit a fairer evaluation. In fact, in many cases, the numbers are perfectly illusory. While the nominal membership lists remain fairly substantial, we saw earlier that American Masons, quite often, after entering the lodge, or as we would say "following their initiation," are hardly diligent in their attendance. Rarely are members removed from the rolls for lack of diligence, and this is already a non-negligible element of distortion in the analysis of statistics in comparison with those of European Masonry. It is, therefore, important to focus our attention not so much on the number of brothers the grand lodges boast but rather on the broad tendencies that Paul Bessel's studies have revealed.

Today, numbers would rather have the tendency to make way for quality, as shown by the debates conducted by the grand lodges in February 2014. In fact, for the first time they have dared to cross the Rubicon and, as indicated earlier, center their discussions on formerly taboo subjects. For example, they are assigning themselves the mission of working together to restore a civic spirit and claim the role of moral compass by placing Masonic virtues in the forefront. Freemasons are thus becoming players in the social debate, claiming their vocation is to be some sort of think tank and announcing the plan to make themselves heard in the agora, so as to make a difference!

What is happening today is not the result of simple chance. What is at work here is that American Freemasons have attained duties on which they have founded their ambition to commit the Order to a path of renewal and openness based on unadulterated Andersonian fundamentals. Already, in discussions between the Grand Lodge of California and myself in May 2013, mention was made of reorientations that caught my attention. In fact, "observance lodges" have recently appeared on the scene. Their distinguishing feature resides in practices that are strangely close to those of lodges in France: the introduction of "boards" and oaths that had been totally prohibited before in the United States; passage through the Chamber of Reflection before initiations, which are not only an "entry" into the lodge; boards of initiation impressions; instruction cycles for apprentices, journeymen, and masters with the help of teaching software on a special Internet site (to make up for the inadequacies of the officials who should fulfill this duty and are not always capable); and an increase in the duration between moving to higher grades. However, all conflictive discussions remain prohibited in the lodge. They take place in the wet room and are already no longer restrained only to aspects of symbolism. This cannot help but open the way to an ad libitum consideration of social questions.

This rule had not yet been retained at the conference in Baltimore at the beginning of 2014, but it cropped up everywhere in discussions. And even if delegates at that time did not adopt the suggestion for a vote by the grand masters on a resolution regarding this direction, we are clearly witnessing a significant reorientation today. It will influence the historical direction of American Freemasonry, which has just taken a significant step. Despite doctrinal differences, this offers a platform on which all Masons (whom I will simply label as those of goodwill) can work together. This is far from a trivial change when we know that the classic American system barely encourages the work in the sense that we understand it. The only thing that counted until this time was the *inner temple*. Most often, entry into Masonry translates into a couple formalities, and the discharge of a modest capitation for life guarantees one continues to appear on lodge rolls without any obligation for diligence or even attendance at a meeting. Under these conditions, just what would the nominal membership numbers presented earlier actually mean?

Those who rub shoulders with the top officials of the obediences and jurisdictions of the American high grades like the Scottish Rite Research Society of the Southern Jurisdiction, as well as the American brothers of the strictest and most demanding symbolic lodges, will qualify their judgments. These fraternal relationships outside the temple give us grounds to confirm the great intellectual and moral qualities of our "separate brothers" as well as their often quite enviable degree of erudition. They make no secret of their ambitions to work for a renewal entirely worthy of the American traditions that the famous phrase "Yes we can" sums up so well and to also provide the means necessary for its realization. There are more than simple subtleties here that should commit everyone to be more attentive to this. As we can see, on a more global level, Masonic movements that can be compared to the shifting of tectonic plates. These are all excellent reasons to not let internal biases get in the way of what is actually happening in the North American Masonic galaxy here and now.

But the stakes in play are already leading us to tomorrow. I have just sketched out some of the principal considerations that should concern us, relying on recent objective data. To return to the present and pursue thoughts of the estrangement from which American Masonry is suffering in all its parts, and this is not to dismiss anything from the preceding observations, let's stop for a moment and look at the possible factors for the origin of this estrangement.

The absence in all American lodges of any analytical debate touching on civil society—and the uncoupling that results in relation to this—could clearly constitute, outside any other consideration, the beginning of an answer to the veritable crisis of diligence and the vocation of initiation that is crisscrossing the majority of American lodges. Hence, the major interest aroused by the reorientations mentioned earlier. The extremely constraining and restrictive reading of Anderson's *Constitutions* and Landmarks, as well as of their obligations, by the American grand lodges (of which we can also sense a still-stuttering beginning of an ad libitum reading) forms a powerful brake to the extent that no debate on fundamentals can be introduced into the lodge.

Even though the history I have unspooled in clips, and certain cultural indicators, have allowed me to explain American Masonic intralodge discourse (or lack thereof), it is so out of sync with how contemporary American society operates on a tradition in which ideas are debated that it cannot help but come as an even greater surprise to the outside observer. This is likely one of the decisive factors for the disinterest that translates into a shortfall of requests for joining and chronic absenteeism. With the exception of a few avant-garde lodges (and they do exist), we are only beginning to detect the shudders that still have trouble finding expression in the resolutions of the obediences, as we have seen confirmed in the last Conference of Grand Masters.

A fainthearted conservatism, which stands out in stark contrast to the innovative spirit of the society taken as a whole, has taken possession of American Freemasonry. It therefore labors against a younger generation of a more cosmopolitan mind-set. The weight of the old guard, and to a certain extent the United Grand Lodge of England ("Keeper of the Truth") as well, forms an obstacle that has yet to be surmounted. Resolutely launching an attack here would presume a ferocious desire to attain that. Woe to those today who expose themselves by acting too audaciously and find themselves defenseless and working in a minefield! Who, moreover, would want to do this? It is this realistic attitude and this freely and reasonably adopted restraint that makes it possible to better grasp the slow pace of the developments that have been triggered. They need to be considered over the long term. We should never lose sight of the sociocultural context permeating American Freemasons, whose rhythms are different from those of European Masons.

If we tackle the Masonic question from the angle of international relations, this slow evolution is a source of hope as it heralds a leap forward, as does the realization—by some of the youngest brothers on taking on official responsibilities—that a common legacy and universally shared initiatory values truly do exist independent of the evolution of specific doctrines for the different obediences. This is something we have seen by analyzing the principal signals that have been revealed by the matter of research, and scholarship in particular.

Still, timidly but realistically, an informal dialogue has been unfolding, initially brother to brother. There are some 150 Masons of the GODF working in the five chapters of this obedience in the United States and Canada, especially those of the high grades of the Ancient and Accepted Scottish Rite. These Masons are particularly well positioned for historical reasons, and, appropriate to the rite (which can easily be labeled Franco-America throughout its history), they have a natural part in this. They are better armed to foresee, sense, and observe, but most importantly to become partners in the possible developments.

The men and women of the GLFB to the Grand Lodge George Washington Union who work in concert with the North American obediences with which they have established friendships will also have their role to play here.

The purpose of these contacts is historical research, exchanges, joint publications, conversations, and sometimes even a white robe meeting open to outsiders when a lodge feels sufficiently bold. I have seen and experienced such experimental actions conducted in the field over the past twenty years, without any useless media racket, but also without any grounds to make them a mystery. I was invited by the lodge Potomac n° 5 of the Washington, D.C., orient as a speaker to deliver an opening address, something that the American brothers were not accustomed to but which they allowed and welcomed with more than simple curiosity. It would not be an exaggeration to say that this was a non-negligible turning point and the start of a reciprocal consideration. I have also mentioned the seminars that the Grand Lodge of California has held since the beginning of the previous decade.

From the East Coast to the West Coast, windows are opening this way. For the first time in a long time, dialogue has been opened by timidly avoiding the doctrinal issues that are a source of irritation. None of these sporadic initiatives have taken as an objective the search for institutional recognition. The innovation of this original dialogue is deliberately situated in a timeless space following the example of the approach taken by Albert Pike in his era. He was the wisest of the wise, an incontestable bearer of a universalist Masonic ambition that has gone astray in the meanderings of a long Masonic river in which he encountered so many shoals. The various entities and "Masonic streams," as our American friends like to say, have evolved like the societies that carried them. There has been a drift of Masonic obediences and jurisdictions just as there was once a drift of continents.

We know from Senegalese anthropologist Cheikh Anta Diop that African man set off to spread over all the continents, of which he gradually took possession by adapting to their different environments. The French anthropologist Claude Lévi-Strauss opened our minds to the fruitful intermixing of men and their cultures. Galileo, although forced to abjure, also taught us that the Earth revolved, no matter what the doctrines of a given time said. Freemasons, perhaps more spontaneously than all men, would be well inspired to learn to take possession of their space in a world that is more multipolar and polymorphous than ever and to learn to live in harmony with the universal principles that have been the foundation of their approach since the beginnings of the seventeenth century.

Masonic families are certainly born from the evolutions experienced during what will soon be three centuries. The plasticity of liberated Masonic thought renders distinguishing features consubstantial to our approach; if it is a source of wealth through the diversity of opinions, it is also the source of our weakness when we have the ambition, with the best intentions in the world, to "gather what has been scattered." Obediences and jurisdictions therefore assert that the regularity and sovereignty of each of them is legitimate. Taking this into consideration, each of them lives the way it deems best in its narrow sociopolitical, cultural, and geopolitical environment.

It would definitely be fanciful to set one's heart on seeing everyone find agreement on a unique body of doctrine, which would be that of a reductive Masonic orthodoxy. It cannot exist, because instead of being the center of union, it would be the smallest common denominator. On the other hand, the Masonic heritage, rich through its great diversity, forms a common platform on which, proceeding by touch, tomorrow's Freemasons of goodwill could build. In this way they could contribute together toward the improvement of the individual and society, but each in his own way, in the full respect of identities and on the duration of a long history. Don't we say when forming our chain of union that we are enrolling into the lineage of the ancestors who preceded us? They are our ancestors, whom we all revere, the "children of the widow." Let us make it so the universal chain of union is made richer with new links, and those who follow us will enter the richness of their fruitful variety. American Freemasonry reveals so much potential that there is no reason to skimp on it.

French and American Freemasons, let's not forget the heritage bequeathed us by Lafayette and Benjamin Franklin! It is high time that we became more productive together by sharing our common legacy as well as our fine and generous ambitions with all Masons of good will!

AFTERWORD

Freemasonry in North America

By John L. Cooper III

Bro.·. Alain de Keghel is eminently qualified to write about North American Freemasonry, having lived and worked in the United States with the French Diplomatic Service. Although universal in nature, Freemasonry bears the imprint of the society in which it exists, and Freemasonry in North America is no exception. American Freemasonry, in particular, was deeply influenced by the colonial and postcolonial experience of the close association of many of the early political leaders with Freemasonry, which led to the intertwining of American Freemasonry with American public life. This experience lent credibility to Freemasonry that it lacked in other societies, and this despite the split of American Freemasonry along racial lines, which still persists. Other characteristics of American Freemasonry are noted, such as the involvement of the families of Freemasons in organizations associated with Freemasonry. While very few women in the United States are involved with women's Freemasonry, the wives and daughters of American Masons are often involved in America's version of adoptive Masonry, the Order of the Eastern Star, and similar organizations. In addition, there are youth organizations that are closely associated with Freemasonry in North America, with lodges sponsoring and actively supporting Masonic-inspired orders for both boys and girls.

American Freemasonry in particular has long had a complicated relationship with French Freemasonry. On the one hand, it honors French Masonic heroes such as Lafayette and remembers that it was the French Masonic community that was instrumental in obtaining French support for the American Revolution. On the other hand, American Freemasonry remains deeply religious and looks with suspicion on any kind of Freemasonry that is not similarly religious. This has resulted in an ambiguous attitude on the part of American Freemasons toward Freemasonry in France, which is explored in this book.

Bro.·. de Keghel's book is a valuable addition to the understanding of Freemasonry in North America in general and in the United States in particular. It is a pleasure to write the afterword for an important addition to the world of Masonic scholarship.

JOHN L. COOPER III

JOHN L. COOPER III was the grand master of Masons in California in 2013–2014 and chairman of the Conference of Grand Masters of Masons in North America in 2014.

Appendices

Contents

Appendix I

Statistical Studies of the Evolution of the Membership of American and Canadian Grand Lodges

MASTER MASONS IN THE U.S. SINCE 1924

The Masonic Service Association has compiled the following table of totals of master Masons in the United States grand lodges for the fiscal years indicated. These figures are based on Masonic Service Association records and do not necessarily correspond exactly with those published by other sources.

YEAR	U.S. TOTAL	YEAR	U.S. TOTAL
1924	3,077,161	1951	3,726,744
1925	3,157,566	1952	3,808,364
1926	3,218,375	1953	3,893,530
1927	3,267,241	1954	3,964,118
1928	3,295,872	1955	4,009,925
1929	3,295,125	1956	4,053,323
1930	3,279,778	1957	4,085,676
1931	3,216,307	1958	4,099,928
1932	3,069,645	1959*	4,103,161
1933	2,901,758	1960	4,099,219
1934	2,760,451	1961	4,086,499
1935	2,659,218	1962	4,063,563
1936	2,591,309	1963	4,034,020
1937	2,549,772	1964	4,005,605
1938	2,514,595	1965	3,987,690
1939	2,482,291	1966	3,948,193
1940	2,457,263	1967	3,910,509
1941	2,451,301	1968	3,868,854
1942	2,478,892	1969	3,817,846
1943	2,561,844	1970	3,763,213
1944	2,719,607	1971	3,718,718
1945	2,896,343	1972	3,661,507
1946	3,097,713	1973	3,611,448
1947	3,281,371	1974	3,561,767
1948	3,426,155	1975	3,512,628
1949	3,545,757	1976	3,470,980
1950	3,644,634	1977	3,418,844

* Indicates highest total

MASTER MASONS IN THE U.S. SINCE 1924 (*cont.*)

YEAR	U.S. TOTAL	YEAR	U.S. TOTAL
1978	3,360,409	1997	2,021,909
1979	3,304,334	1998	1,967,208
1980	3,251,528	1999	1,902,588
1981	3,188,175	2000	1,841,169
1982	3,121,746	2001	1,774,200
1983	3,060,242	2002	1,727,505
1984	2,992,389	2003	1,671,255
1985	2,914,421	2004	1,617,032
1986	2,839,962	2005	1,569,812
1987	2,763,828	2006	1,525,131
1988	2,682,537	2007	1,483,449
1989	2,608,935	2008	1,444,823
1990	2,531,643	2009	1,404,059
1991	2,452,676	2010	1,373,453
1992	2,371,863	2011	1,336,503
1993	2,293,949	2012	1,306,539
1994	2,225,611	2013	1,246,241
1995	2,153,316	2014	1,211,183
1996	2,089,578	2015**	1,161,253

**Indicates lowest point

MASONIC MEMBERSHIP IN THE UNITED STATES, 1925–2010

(from Masonic Service Association of North America statistics)

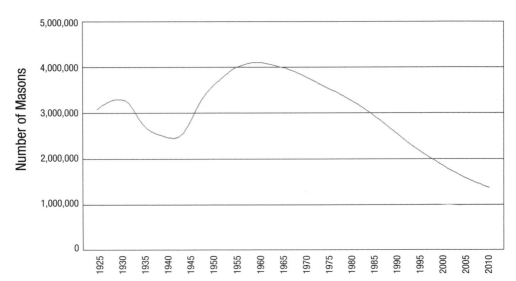

U.S. GRAND LODGES MEMBERSHIP

STATE	MEMBERSHIP 2011	MEMBERSHIP 2012	GAIN/ LOSS
ALABAMA *	27,576	27,654	78
ALASKA	1,868	1,820	-48
ARIZONA	8,263	8,000	-263
ARKANSAS *	12,005	13,042	1,037
CALIFORNIA *	57,250	63,546	6,296
COLORADO	9,320	8,885	-435
CONNECTICUT	12,423	11,778	-645
DELAWARE	4,997	4,910	-87
DISTRICT OF COLUMBIA *	4,424	4,438	14
FLORIDA	44,437	42,959	-1478
GEORGIA	42,297	41,255	-1042
HAWAII	1,806	1,778	-28
IDAHO	3,832	3,682	-150
ILLINOIS	66,347	65,781	-566
INDIANA	62,968	60,449	-2519
IOWA	20,844	20,203	-641
KANSAS	22,004	21,225	-779
KENTUCKY	45,275	43,658	-1617
LOUISIANA	20,482	20,404	-78
MAINE	21,033	19,860	-1173
MARYLAND *	15,998	16,146	148
MASSACHUSETTS	35,333	33,048	-2285
MICHIGAN	36,172	34,686	-1486
MINNESOTA	14,084	13,587	-497
MISSISSIPPI	18,689	18,063	-626
MISSOURI	50,415	45,850	-4565
MONTANA	5,773	5,597	-176
NEBRASKA	12,271	11,895	-376
NEVADA	4,168	4,163	-5
NEW HAMPSHIRE	6,681	6,496	-185
NEW JERSEY	23,209	22,523	-686
NEW MEXICO	5,590	5,389	-201
NEW YORK	44,776	42,669	-2107
NORTH CAROLINA	43,644	43,112	-532
NORTH DAKOTA	2,927	2,876	-51
OHIO	101,929	94,867	-7062
OKLAHOMA	24,068	23,842	-226
OREGON	9,203	8,946	-257

* Increase over 2011

U.S. GRAND LODGES MEMBERSHIP (*cont.*)

STATE	MEMBERSHIP 2011	MEMBERSHIP 2012	GAIN/ LOSS
PENNSYLVANIA	111,661	108,758	-2903
RHODE ISLAND	4,161	3,573	-588
SOUTH CAROLINA	38,853	37,811	-1042
SOUTH DAKOTA	5,902	5,679	-223
TENNESSEE	43,015	41,780	-1235
TEXAS *	88,896	93,188	4292
UTAH *	2,034	2,057	23
VERMONT	6,299	5,855	-444
VIRGINIA	38,008	37,177	-831
WASHINGTON	16,110	15,450	-660
WEST VIRGINIA	21,242	20,808	-434
WISCONSIN	12,165	11,742	-423
WYOMING	3,776	3,579	-197
Total	**1,336,503**	**1,306,539**	**-29,964**

* Increase over 2011

CANADIAN GRAND LODGES MEMBERSHIP

PROVINCE	Membership 2011	Membership 2012	GAIN/ LOSS
ALBERTA	7,336	7,284	-52
BRITISH COLUMBIA	8,882	8,589	-293
MANITOBA	2,502	2,410	-92
NEW BRUNSWICK	3,274	3,154	-120
NEWFOUNDLAND/ LABRADOR	2,128	2,111	-17
NOVA SCOTIA	4,740	4,554	-186
ONTARIO	47,522	45,660	-1,862
PRINCE EDWARD ISLAND	734	722	-12
QUEBEC *	4,172	4,182	10
SASKATCHEWAN	2,892	2,822	-70
Total	**84,182**	**81,488**	**- 2,694**

* Increase over 2011

NUMBER OF MASONS PER U.S. STATE

(from Masonic Service Association of North America statistics)

	1998	1999	2000	2001	2002	2003	2004	2005	2006	2007	2008	2009	2010	1998 to 2010	
AL	42,836	41,038	39,766	38,410	36,436	34,900	33,700	32,297	30,952	29,775	30,122	28,386	28,684	(14,450)	-34%
AK	2,085	2,061	2,029	2,035	1,924	2,050	2,177	2,145	2,053	2,003	1,982	1,935	1,935	(150)	-7%
AZ	11,706	11,500	11,381	11,117	11,130	10,734	10,504	10,210	9,900	9,642	9,315	9,023	8,651	(2,683)	-23%
AR	26,856	23,697	22,126	21,707	20,791	19,278	18,626	17,699	17,082	16,524	16,094	15,027	14,429	(11,829)	-44%
CA	101,173	94,693	90,914	85,520	82,318	78,108	71,827	71,810	68,714	66,127	63,497	58,889	57,267	(42,284)	-42%
CO	18,500	17,745	17,014	16,305	15,737	15,677	14,970	13,737	13,160	12,645	11,421	10,742	10,356	(7,758)	-42%
CT	19,757	18,859	18,276	17,618	17,018	16,497	15,787	15,126	14,543	14,185	13,926	13,432	12,895	(6,325)	-32%
DE	6,308	6,110	6,110	5,952	5,503	5,688	5,591	5,302	5,075	5,111	5,260	5,150	5,110	(1,158)	-18%
DC	5,666	5,464	5,316	5,170	4,986	4,897	4,760	4,642	4,602	4,552	4,434	4,312	4,341	(1,354)	-24%
FL	63,100	61,199	59,689	58,451	57,124	55,306	54,373	51,973	50,829	49,964	48,658	47,471	45,940	(15,629)	-25%
GA	62,166	60,168	58,606	57,091	55,681	52,703	51,036	49,341	47,998	46,914	45,736	44,523	43,578	(17,643)	-28%
HI	2,137	2,198	2,154	2,069	1,906	1,751	1,734	1,745	1,781	1,733	1,733	1,643	1,742	(494)	-23%
ID	6,390	6,131	5,918	5,683	5,463	5,186	4,829	4,688	4,688	4,412	4,225	4,191	3,962	(2,199)	-34%
IL	91,697	88,566	85,712	80,936	77,072	75,526	74,810	72,793	71,241	69,703	68,562	68,308	65,564	(23,389)	-26%
IN	89,278	86,542	84,884	82,230	80,047	78,397	75,845	73,380	71,392	68,759	67,777	66,006	65,443	(23,272)	-26%
IA	33,117	30,940	29,613	28,438	28,109	27,367	26,500	25,697	24,826	23,960	23,140	22,466	21,695	(10,651)	-32%
KS	40,364	37,790	35,900	34,474	33,027	31,507	30,175	28,863	27,674	26,171	25,115	24,091	23,074	(16,273)	-40%
KY	63,426	61,626	59,979	58,057	56,537	54,585	52,729	51,437	50,260	48,955	48,408	47,747	46,362	(15,679)	-25%
LA	27,295	26,551	25,884	25,471	24,792	24,812	24,326	23,666	23,000	22,707	22,006	20,070	21,004	(7,225)	-26%
ME	27,115	26,458	25,873	25,238	24,595	24,021	23,381	22,849	22,281	21,659	20,363	19,968	20,294	(7,147)	-26%
MD	24,280	23,674	22,923	22,155	21,124	20,263	19,667	18,771	18,112	17,608	17,054	16,477	16,235	(7,803)	-32%

NUMBER OF MASONS PER U.S. STATE (cont.)

	1998	1999	2000	2001	2002	2003	2004	2005	2006	2007	2008	2009	2010	1998 to 2010	
MA	53,613	51,542	49,810	43,497	41,972	41,356	39,865	39,209	37,173	37,777	36,848	36,518	35,944	(17,095)	-32%
MI	61,234	58,767	56,366	53,804	51,468	49,701	47,536	45,780	44,131	42,737	41,185	39,189	37,709	(22,045)	-36%
MN	23,051	22,046	21,145	20,304	19,474	18,860	18,051	17,351	16,785	16,262	15,782	15,182	14,721	(7,869)	-34%
MS	28,336	27,370	26,345	25,537	24,768	24,008	23,150	22,418	21,717	21,248	20,493	19,774	19,341	(8,562)	-30%
MO	53,829	55,887	55,341	53,997	53,139	52,061	51,923	51,873	51,858	51,775	51,500	51,000	50,500	(2,829)	-5%
MT	9,208	8,874	8,684	8,413	8,113	7,880	7,647	7,474	7,276	6,985	6,605	6,342	5,990	(2,866)	-31%
NE	18,280	17,633	17,042	16,507	16,180	15,656	15,257	14,840	14,391	13,988	13,498	13,038	12,716	(5,242)	-29%
NV	5,539	5,360	5,357	5,231	5,046	5,051	4,868	4,862	4,656	4,504	4,390	4,316	4,225	(1,223)	-22%
NH	9,297	9,096	8,827	8,615	8,318	8,064	7,844	7,660	7,456	7,279	7,156	6,928	6,898	(2,369)	-25%
NJ	37,264	36,178	34,949	33,707	32,617	31,420	30,885	31,169	29,652	28,579	27,297	26,073	24,775	(11,191)	-30%
NM	7,686	7,498	7,319	7,082	6,812	6,715	6,521	6,085	5,703	5,579	5,211	5,227	5,553	(2,459)	-32%
NY	73,079	69,787	67,403	64,932	62,368	60,889	55,560	52,997	53,097	50,580	49,082	48,051	45,801	(25,028)	-34%
NC	57,989	56,595	55,204	53,805	52,585	50,647	49,659	48,092	47,722	47,137	46,300	45,685	45,096	(12,304)	-21%
ND	4,551	4,270	4,190	3,910	4,004	3,803	3,620	3,560	3,450	3,385	3,269	3,151	3,055	(1,400)	-31%
OH	143,882	138,547	133,599	128,547	131,557	129,628	124,508	120,615	116,761	114,661	110,250	108,332	106,370	(35,550)	-25%
OK	36,946	36,330	34,863	33,804	33,220	33,744	32,585	30,735	29,620	28,713	27,723	26,572	25,739	(10,374)	-28%
OR	15,717	15,124	14,411	13,738	13,237	12,492	11,656	11,559	11,197	10,736	10,330	9,970	9,541	(5,747)	-37%
PA	147,497	144,682	140,057	137,877	133,676	129,916	128,886	125,738	123,276	120,502	117,584	114,447	113,279	(33,050)	-22%
RI	6,424	5,966	5,799	5,593	5,371	5,172	5,111	4,744	4,643	4,490	4,183	4,326	4,213	(2,098)	-33%
SC	53,249	51,851	50,446	49,180	47,913	46,740	45,325	44,278	43,315	42,463	41,597	40,798	39,927	(12,451)	-23%
SD	7,903	7,701	7,497	7,238	7,133	6,978	6,924	6,796	6,658	6,527	6,372	6,262	6,094	(1,641)	-21%
TN	66,747	64,991	62,233	60,815	59,394	57,437	55,464	54,143	51,086	48,677	46,828	46,156	44,691	(20,591)	-31%

NUMBER OF MASONS PER U.S. STATE (cont.)

	1998	1999	2000	2001	2002	2003	2004	2005	2006	2007	2008	2009	2010	98 to 10	
TX	137,425	134,609	132,377	126,870	123,588	112,977	109,532	105,434	101,803	98,398	95,289	92,656	91,632	(44,769)	-33%
UT	2,531	2,455	2,402	2,254	2,183	2,180	2,092	2,070	1,947	1,944	1,963	1,920	2,035	(611)	-24%
VT	8,479	8,292	8,035	7,836	7,631	7,631	7,554	7,342	7,217	7,019	6,823	6,466	6,444	(2,013)	-24%
VA	48,206	47,082	45,995	44,866	43,840	42,853	41,849	41,351	40,546	40,052	39,839	39,238	38,498	(8,968)	-19%
WA	24,862	23,886	23,083	20,081	21,108	20,356	19,624	18,999	18,693	16,372	17,682	17,109	15,369	(7,753)	-31%
WV	28,757	28,079	27,409	26,797	26,128	25,383	24,708	24,047	23,452	22,947	22,557	22,078	21,643	(6,679)	-23%
WI	20,672	19,639	18,869	18,445	17,752	17,024	16,324	15,736	15,117	14,600	14,134	13,328	12,694	(7,344)	-36%
WY	6,503	6,241	6,018	5,818	5,590	5,380	5,157	4,684	4,570	4,424	4,225	4,070	3,899	(2,433)	-37%
Total	1,966,006	1,901,387	1,843,142	1,775,228	1,729,507	1,673,258	1,619,036	1,571,817	1,527,137	1,485,456	1,446,831	1,406,068	1,375,463	(559,938)	-28%

PERCENTAGE OF U.S. MEMBERSHIP LOSSES, 1998–2010

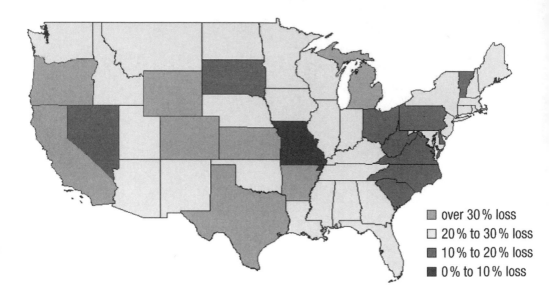

- ▨ over 30% loss
- ☐ 20% to 30% loss
- ▩ 10% to 20% loss
- ■ 0% to 10% loss

AVERAGE ANNUAL DECREASE IN PERCENTAGE OF U.S. MASONS FROM 1994 TO 2005
TOTAL AVERAGE: 3%

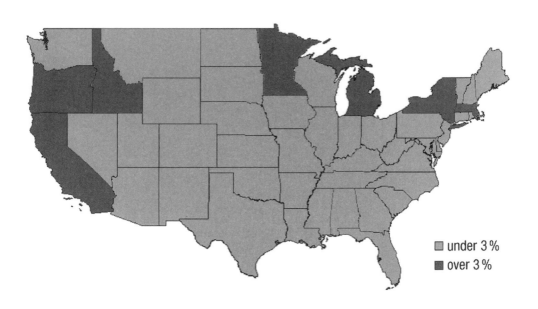

- ▨ under 3%
- ■ over 3%

NUMBER OF MASONS BY STATE IN 2003

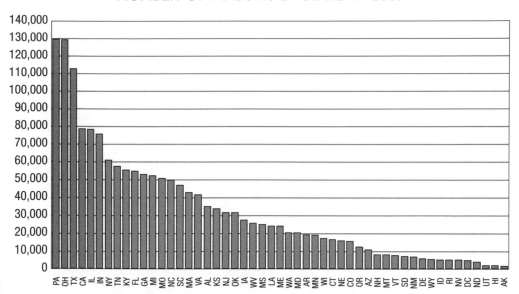

LOSS OF MASONIC ACTIVE MEMBERS
FROM 1998 TO 2010

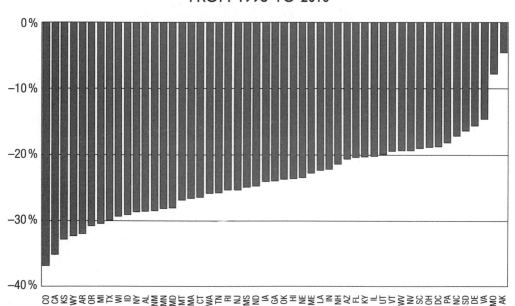

NUMBER OF MASONS IN "PREDOMINANTLY WHITE"
(NON–PRINCE HALL) GRAND LODGES
IN EACH U.S. STATE IN 2005

(from Masonic Service Association of North America statistics)

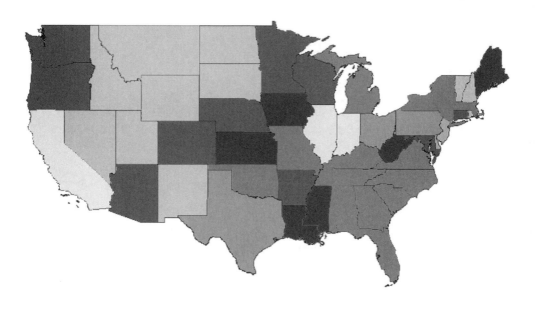

- ▨ 0 to 10,000
- ■ 10,000 to 20,000
- ■ 20,000 to 30,000
- ▨ 30,000 to 60,000
- ☐ 60,000 to 100,000
- ▨ 100,000 to 150,000

NUMBER OF MASONS IN PROPORTION TO THE POPULATION OF EACH STATE IN 2005

(from Masonic Service Association of North America statistics)

Note: Some Grand Lodges count multiple members only once, some count multiple members as many times as the number of lodges to which they belong.

State	Number of Masons (does not include Prince Hall Masons)	Total population 7/1/05 according to U.S. Census Bureau
AL	32,297	4,557,808
AK	2,145	663,661
AZ	10,210	5,939,292
AR	17,699	2,779,154
CA	71,810	36,132,147
CO	13,737	4,665,177
CT	15,126	3,510,297
DE	5,302	843,524
DC	4,642	550,521
FL	51,973	17,789,864
GA	49,341	9,072,576
HI	1,745	1,275,194
ID	4,688	1,429,096
IL	72,793	12,763,371
IN	73,380	6,271,973
IA	25,697	2,966,334
KS	28,863	2,744,687
KY	51,437	4,173,405
LA	23,666	4,523,628
ME	22,849	1,321,505
MD	18,771	5,600,388
MA	39,209	6,398,743
MI	45,780	10,120,860
MN	17,351	5,132,799
MS	22,418	2,921,088
MO	51,873	5,800,310
MT	7,474	935,670
NE	14,840	1,758,787

NUMBER OF MASONS IN PROPORTION TO THE POPULATION OF EACH STATE IN 2005 (*cont.*)

State	Number of Masons (does not include Prince Hall Masons)	Total population 7/1/05 according to U.S. Census Bureau
NV	4,862	2,414,807
NH	7,660	1,309,940
NJ	31,169	8,717,925
NM	6,085	1,928,384
NY	52,997	19,254,630
NC	48,092	8,683,242
ND	3,560	636,677
OH	120,615	11,464,042
OK	30,735	3,547,884
OR	11,559	3,641,056
PA	125,738	12,429,616
RI	4,744	1,076,189
SC	44,278	4,255,083
SD	6,796	775,933
TN	54,143	5,962,959
TX	105,434	22,859,968
UT	2,070	2,469,585
VT	7,342	623,050
VA	41,351	7,567,465
WA	18,999	6,287,759
WV	24,047	1,816,856
WI	15,736	5,536,201
WY	4,684	509,294
Total	**1,569,812**	**296,410,404**

http://bessel.org/masstats.hm
Copyright © 1998-2014 by Paul M. Bessel – all rights reserved

Appendix II

American Demographic Studies

Sources: U.S. Census Bureau and the *Washington Post*

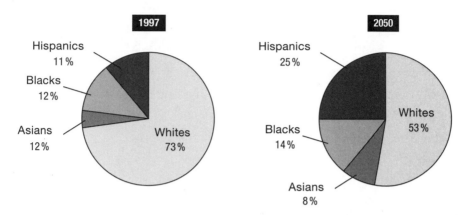

Demographic projections: The "Asian" category includes the residents of the Pacific Islands; other races are less than 1 percent of the total.

Since 1978, the U.S. federal government, with its *Federal Directive No. 15,* has officially recognized four ethnic and racial groups.

1. American Indian or Alaskan Native: A person having origins in any of the original peoples of North America and who maintains cultural identification through tribal affiliation or community recognition.

2. Asian or Pacific Islander: A person having origins in any of the original peoples of the Far East, Southeast Asia, the Indian subcontinent, or the Pacific Islands. This area includes, for example, China, India, Japan, Korea, the Philippine Islands, and Samoa.

3. Black: A person having origins in any of the black racial groups of Africa.

4. Hispanic: A person of Mexican, Puerto Rican, Cuban, Central or South American, or other Spanish-speaking culture or origin, regardless of race. The term *Hispanic* is the one used officially by

the federal authorities (census data, forms, etc.), but the community often prefers the term *Latino,* which sounds less European. The U.S. government considers Hispanics as an ethnic group, which means there are white Hispanics and those of darker skin color.

Federal Directive No. 15 was revised at the beginning of the year 2000 to include five racial categories by dividing the second category as follows: Asians on the one side and on the other Native Hawaiians and other Pacific Islanders.

Appendix III

*Speech on the Occasion of the
Commemoration of the Twentieth Anniversary
of the Lighting of the Fires (May 3, 2009)*

Bo∴ of Bro∴ Alain de Keghel, Former Venerable Master of the W∴ L∴ La Fayette 89, Or∴ of Washington

In 2007, the Supreme Council of the Ancient and Accepted Scottish Rite of the Grand Orient of France decided to share, during the time of my chairmanship, the commemorative duty of going to Picpus Cemetery in Paris and laying a wreath. This was the way the Grand Orient of France recognized the part the marquis de Lafayette had played during that tumultuous period when freedom was won as a fruit of the Enlightenment.

It was during this same time and for the same reasons that a pamphlet was published in homage to this brother who portrayed the idea of liberty as the Grail and gave the tone of a crusade to his actions, and who had at his command a veritable genius for coining phrases, inspiring Sainte-Beuve to write, "His language was made in his design."

"America" wrote Axelle de Gaigneron in a text dedicated to General Lafayette in 1996, "projected upon him a symbolic vision of its own creation—half way between myth and folk imagery. So much so that an entire aspect of his life, perpetuated by an art that switched between pompous and naïve, unfolded before the eyes of memory from one stage to the next 'like a saga, the saga of the Lafayettides.'" This is the saga to which Americans make sacrifice every year on July 4 when they make their way to pay him homage at the Parisian cemetery of Picpus.

Mainly celebrated as a hero of American independence, Lafayette was also an extremely active Freemason. And it is this perhaps less well-known aspect that deserves to be seen today, the day on which we are commemorating the lighting of the fires of our respectable lodge that proudly bears his name. This is because his Masonic commitment was equally decisive in his options on behalf of the rebels' cause. Although neither the exact date nor the lodge of his initiation have been established, the Acts of the Grand Lodge of Tennessee of May 4, 1825, cited in a book by William Denslow, mentions, on the faith of Brother Lafayette's own statements, that he entered Freemasonry in France long before he arrived in the United States of America.

Some authors, without offering any concrete proof, have believed they could state that Lafayette was initiated into the R. L. La Candeur on December 25, 1775. As it happens, consultation of the archives of this Masonic lodge proves that while his name does indeed appear on its log this day, he took part in the proceedings as a visitor.

Despite the lack of formal proof for this hypothesis, it is nonetheless highly likely and generally accepted by historians that he was initiated at the age of eighteen in 1775 into a military lodge while he was serving at the garrison of Metz. It was moreover in Metz, during a dinner given by the comte de Broglie to the Duke of Gloucester, brother of the King of England, that Gilbert du Motier, the marquis de Lafayette, first heard about the American rebels and he recalled that moment by stating, "My heart was enlisted." This was how the "great simpleton whose mind was as pale as his face," according to the murderous phrase of his contemporary, Armand d'Allonville, entered his American epic.

His membership in Freemasonry is not foreign to this twist of fate, for on his arrival in Paris he immediately rubbed shoulders with the brother Benjamin Franklin, then venerable master of the famous Lodge of the Nine Sisters. This very famous American had arrived in Paris in 1776 as an extraordinary ambassador. He then secretly planned to leave for America, where in 1778 Lafayette declared before the American Congress, "From the first moment I heard spoken the name of America, I loved it; from the moment I learned that it was fighting for freedom, I burned with the desire to spill my blood for her; the days when I can serve it will be numbered among the happiest of my life in all times and all places."

The personal and fraternal relationship between Lafayette and George Washington has given birth to much fantasizing. It deserves better than the legend. Even if we hear Washington say of him, when the young Lafayette had just been wounded at the Battle of Brandywine in September 1777,

"Treat him as my own son, for I love him as if he were my own," the tone is primarily paternalistic. In fact, this phrase of the father of his country, which has gone down in history, should not conjure up a false picture. And yet, today the two names are almost inseparable and practically equal in the American imagination. As they are in ours, as we have chosen it to be a Masonic reference as a strong symbol of Franco-American bonds.

Lafayette's Masonic life was decisive in his saga, through his relations in the lodge with Franklin first, then, as we shall see, with Brother Washington. Several authors in the United States have, despite Lafayette's own statements on this subject and in complete contradiction with the evidence, put forth the notion that he was initiated on December 29, 1779, in Morristown, New Jersey. It is quite plausible and more convincing that, as at Valley Forge, where he attended with Brother George Washington the Respectable Lodge the American Union during the winter of 1777–1778, he formed ties with the American lodges that his travels there led him to frequent. This would obviously explain his name appearing in the lists of those present. Mentioning this in 1825, Lafayette observed with his characteristic emphasis, "After I was made a Mason, General Washington seemed to have received a new light. I never had from that moment any cause to doubt his entire confidence." This was a moment of great lucidity concerning the time before this illumination when, for all intents and purposes, as can be seen in the letters between the two men, the trust granted the young brother by Washington was not always complete nor without shades of gray.

In France it has been established that he was linked to and therefore a member of the Respectable Lodge Saint Jean d'Écosse du Contrat Social [Saint John of Scotland of the Social Contract] in the Orient of Paris on June 24, 1782, and that in 1806 he was the sitting venerable master of the Respectable Lodge Les Amis de la Verité in the Orient of Rosay en Brie. After 1815 his Masonic activity was one with his commitment to the Bourbon Restoration. On the pretext of visiting the lodges, he organized a vast movement in favor of the Liberal Party. To a certain extent he was the first figure to make Masonry a political, or more precisely, partisan vehicle, in favor of the ideas of the progress of man and society.

Nevertheless, his role during the French Revolution has led historians to introduce some gray areas into the judgments laid down by his hagiographers. Lafayette appeared as a figure of many facets, and John Adams, future second president of the United States, wrote about him in 1790 that he "saw in this young idol a boundless ambition, we should be wary. . . . He entered our service very young and held a position of high command at which he succeeded, but he received more acclaim than a young man of his age could stand." Nor is the personal part he played in the drafting of the Declaration of the Rights of Man, or that in the writing of the Edict on the Protestants, unknown.

Before that time, on his return to France in 1781, Lafayette had also dared to venture a suggestion that draws from the roots of his Masonic humanism but which was quickly deemed absurd in America. At this time he had taken an interest in the condition of slaves, but without going so far as to envision the abolition of this institution in the United States. Following a "vagabond" itinerary, Lafayette would basically be eternally captive to a boundless personal ambition that would inevitably stain his image. It was only in Masonry where this aspect of his character did not manifest, but this is not a space where the stakes of power are wagered. At best it permitted him a communion of thought with several enlightened minds who shared his infatuation for freedom. This space of open sociability suited him quite well.

Lafayette's entrance into the high grades of the Ancient and Accepted Scottish Rite took place in 1830 under the auspices of the Supreme Council of the Grand Orient of France during the reign of Louis-Philippe. Outside of his extensive Masonic correspondence with the brothers of the rite belonging in particular to the Respectable Lodge La Constante Amitié in the Orient of Paris, there is no prominent evidence of his particular activity in this regard. However, in a book published in 1935 under the title *La Fayette ou le militant Franc-maçon,* author André Lebey describes him as a very active brother, and it is enough to read Lafayette's veritable act of faith to be entirely convinced of his idealistic virtues. On June 7, 1777, he sent a letter to his wife in which he says, "Whilst defending the liberty I adore, I will enjoy perfect freedom myself; I offer my services to that interesting republic from motives of the purest kind. The happiness of America is intimately connected with the happiness of all mankind; she will become the safe and respected asylum of virtue, integrity, tolerance, equality, and a tranquil freedom."

In Lyon, Lafayette paid two visits to Masonic lodges, and both visits were described by Pierre Piovesan, former high speaker of the Scottish Jurisdiction of the GODF, in an article published in 2003 in the book *Lyon, carrefour européen de la Franc-maçonnerie* on the occasion of the exhibition and event at the Fine Arts Museum there to celebrate the 275th anniversary of Freemasonry in France.

It was much later that the Sovereign Grand Cerneau Consistory, the dissident jurisdiction of New York, in rupture with that of Charleston, finally made Lafayette grand inspector general of the 33rd and final degree of the Ancient and Accepted Scottish Rite, during his last trip to America. An episode that does not figure on the less stormy pages of an institutional Franco-American Masonic relationship whose complexity historians know full well. And as we know so well, it remains one today.

The George Washington Masonic National Memorial in Alexandria owns and displays a Masonic apron that is supposed to have been embroidered by Adrienne de Lafayette and offered by our compatriot to George Washington. But nothing confirms the authenticity of this piece. On the other hand, the Museum of the Grand Orient of France has on display a very handsome and authentic Masonic sword belonging to Lafayette. With its gilded bronze guard inscribed with Masonic decorations, its mother-of-pearl hilt, and its "flamboyant" blade, this magnificent ceremonial sword goes back to the last years of the Empire or the first years of the Restoration. It is one of the most beautiful and precious jewels of the museum. Furthermore, one of the most prestigious temples of the headquarters of the Grand Orient of France bears the name Lafayette. Its tri-colored décor evokes the emergence of the Republic and admirably echoes Lafayette's creation of the cockade.

As former venerable master, the third in order of seniority of the R. L. La Fayette 89 of the Orient of Washington, I am happy to have been invited to testify to this great day celebrating the anniversary of our respectable lodge, of the complete way in which this prestigious Mason so valiantly took up the defense, with all the nuances you just heard, of the high fundamental values and grand ideals of freedom, as well as the hopes for the betterment of man and society, which are dearest to us. He was able to fortunately combine a militant Masonic life with an uncommon degree of political and military activity. He deserves our special homage as well as the duty to remember him. Let us show proof at his place of the goodwill with which the hindsight of history and the fraternity inspires us, and thus recognition.

May this modest board remain as one of the testimonies of this long line of ancestors that connects us both in space and time, the chain of fraternal union that shall never break.

ALAIN DE KEGHEL

FORMER VENERABLE MASTER

(1995–1996 AND 1996–1997)

Appendix IV

*Sacramento Seminar of 2002, Organized by the
Grand Lodge of California*

Speech of Alain de Keghel at the Franco-American Masonic Seminar of Sacramento

. . . The time has come to speak.

The time has come to engage fraternally in a deep and sustained analysis of the international Masonic landscape. All Brethren of goodwill are looking toward a more open-minded, more tolerant, and more Masonic approach to our Brotherhood. To that end, increasing numbers of Masons from around the world are making the necessary efforts to build a bridge of light. It is a bridge of light that does not end at national borders or within the institutional limits of Masonic bodies wheresoever they might be found around the world. It is a bridge that is built in order to overcome prejudices, and to open eyes, minds, and hearts to the inherited legacies of our diverse and rich traditions.

It is indeed a great privilege and rare opportunity to gather with brethren of the five continents in order to share different experiences and to try to open more widely the doors of understanding. So let us attempt to overcome the friction of difference that far too often marks the realities of the profane world, and as a consequence also tarnishes our Masonic world. We should do this not for the unworthy goal of Masonic proselytizing, but simply to attempt a modest dialogue between men and Masons of goodwill, between brethren of distinct *Masonic streams* that are each, in fact, a lasting source of treasure. Why? We do it because similar efforts have always strengthened our spiritual, philosophical, philanthropic, and traditional Order.

The Masonic order has endured through the vicissitudes of time, culture, civilizations, and society. However, it has survived through the centuries not by passively following the movements of civil society, but rather it often has been at the forefront of change within society.

This is necessary because it is our duty to test our discrimination and open our minds toward the future of the Masonic order at the turn of the twenty-first century and of the third millennium. However, in order to do this adequately, it is obvious that we first need to know each other much better than we do.

To be direct and to the point, I will first offer a few words concerning the Grand Orient of France: No, it is not a communist organization! No, it has not relinquished the Great Architect of the Universe. No, it has never initiated women. *But . . .*

Yes, it is the oldest traditional Masonic body in France, and its very strong commitment in the establishment of Freemasonry in the early years of Latin America and elsewhere is well documented.

Yes, the Grand Orient, with more than forty-two thousand brethren, is the largest French Masonic organization in a country that counts a total of roughly 120,000 men as members working in a lodge.

You, of course, realize that Freemasonry developed in a different way in France as well as in many other countries. There is no need to lock ourselves into unnecessary compartments and singular ways of thinking. We need to be concerned about the weakness that results from unnecessary divisions. We would be much wiser to prefer a universal perspective, because our way of thinking is a legacy of the great philosophers and writers of the time of the Enlightenment: Voltaire, Rousseau, Montesquieu, Diderot, and before them of individuals such as Ephraim Chambers, with his *Encyclopedia or Dictionary of the Arts and Sciences,* first published in 1728. We must leave the heritage of our humanist and Enlightenment values to future generations.

The essential point is that our Masonic message is still of value. The great, generous, and original ideal of Freemasonry to "unite people who otherwise would have remained at perpetual distance" is also a modern and vital message to our contemporary society endangered by egoism, ethnocentrism, and crude materialism. At this time, everyone is speaking of globalization. But where are we as Freemasons in the contemporary world? Are we not at risk in our current situation? Is it not possible that the world will pass us by in the new millennium if we do not actively engage with humanity once again and give the message that is expected from us?

It is precisely our rules and regulations that make a universal dialogue among all Freemasons virtually impossible. Is it not a kind of a paradox that today the Roman Catholic Church has lifted the excommunication of Freemasons, but Freemasons of different disciplines in fact excommunicate each other? Is this a sane and normal situation?

Having always made this argument, and being supportive of constructive change, I notice in this regard that some significant changes are beginning to occur.

Of course, none of us today has a miraculous "ready-made" solution to suggest. We can only work to find a solution step-by-step. That is how we can all be pragmatic and helpful. The first step is simply *to take into consideration the simple truth that there are different Masonic streams.* Each of these traditions reflects specific historical, sociological, cultural, religious, spiritual, and national realities. We need to take them into account, as they are, and not as we think they should be. No one of us is so privileged with wisdom that it would entitle us to enforce a universal Masonic creed. But we can see the result today of closed and self-righteous thinking. It is very frustrating to all of us. Practically, we have to abandon any illusion or vain hope to change the remarkable and healthy diversity in order to reunify Masonic streams.

Starting from this matter of fact, why should we not seriously consider the very real option of becoming more dynamic, more imaginative, more creative and positive in order to develop a new kind of relationship? This would not necessarily imply any kind of formal recognition. It would also not harm our respective rules and regulations and would not lead us to violate any of our solemn obligations. That makes common sense.

Let us take the example of the Roman Catholic Church: it meets and conducts a sophisticated and ambitious dialogue with the other religious communities, but it does not perform church services in which ministers of different disciplines work together ritualistically. In other words, it places its heart, and service, in favor of ecumenism, but this kind of ecumenism and openness does not result in confusion or the violation of obligations for its ministers.

Why could we Freemasons of different lineages not act in a similar way?

We need not attend tyled lodge meetings together. No single French brother from the Grand Orient should ever expect to attend such a stated communication simply because we respect your identity, your specific commitment, your discipline, and your tradition. However, on a reciprocal basis it is possible that we can make progress. It would require tolerance and an open minded spirit. But the time has come to sit together. In one way or another, we need to make sincere efforts to forge new kinds of relationships that are conducive to dialogue. We need adequate mechanisms and tools that enable true Masonic cooperation. It would be easier to use various existing channels: Historians and scholars, for example, could profitably join efforts in building toward mutual understanding and knowledge. Joint working committees could be inaugurated in order to share thoughts on a range of issues outside of the temple and without ritual.

This would be a first step.

Let us work to be a new kind of Freemason. A Freemason who is candid and practical but capable of utopian hopes that have ever been at the heart of real change in society. In fact, to return to the opening part of my remarks, I am speaking about the same type of bold and vital Freemasonry that helped to pave the way to democracy. In our dreams, in our thinking, and in our practical steps, we must move to become active players in life. We stand at the landmark of a new millennium, and we should act and prosper accordingly.

We can recall minding the proposals of the grand commander of the German Scottish Rite, Ill.·. Br.·. Gunter Muenzberg, ten years ago in Mexico City. He stated then that "in a world which has changed so much, Freemasonry must come out of its old shell. . . . Problems have been proclaimed often in recent decades by many farsighted Freemasons, but these problems, and their solutions, have not been incorporated into the strategic thinking of the sclerotic Masonic institutions themselves. . . . The Masonic institutions should present the moral law in appropriate, flexible outer forms. Masonic systems would bring the norms, values, and insights, mainly esoteric, of their Masonic thinking into expression in a contemporary Magna Charta, or rule . . . that would not be dogmatic, rather, it would be flexible and adaptable through time, and place, and yet valid for all Freemasons. This could replace the confusing wide array of misunderstood 'Landmarks' currently in existence.

"Freemasonry is a political factor, whether it wants to be or not. It cannot close its eyes concerning either the environment or the people.

"The Masonic institutions should, of course, not get involved in politics. This would be a blind alley. . . . Bridge building is only possible if the type of institutions that I am speaking about remain neutral. Completely different, however, is the situation of each single Brother. He should participate fully in society, in public life, and especially in the open and tolerant discourses where opinions are formed. Only when we follow these, or similar, paths can we engage in effective service to humanity as a strong, vibrant, diverse, and universal organization. If we do nothing today, in another 10 to 20 years, the call for reformations will be heard even more loudly."

These remarks were made ten years ago in Mexico City. Almost nothing has happened since this desperate cry. This message still resonates today in our ears both as a warning and a legacy.

Let us be the brave brethren who are today able to undertake the difficult tasks of change faithfully, but also with courage and realism. It will be well worth the effort for all of us. When you work toward such goals one thing is certain. You will always be able to rely on brethren of goodwill from around the world, not only in France, in the great Masonic task of building the ever new temple of humanity.

Appendix V

Geneva Declaration
(May 7, 2005)

Preamble

The jurisdictions of higher Scottish degrees, gathering at Geneva from the fifth to the eighth of May 2005, for their Eighteenth International Scottish Meeting, consider that the time has come to mark a new stage after the declaration made at Lausanne a hundred and thirty years ago in a different international Masonic surrounding. They nevertheless refer to this founding text, because it allows the assertion of the everlastingness and universalism of the Masonic principles.

In 1875 the world was dominated by Europe. The nineteenth century was, moreover, characterized by the triumph of the nationalities and the summit of glory of nation-states fenced in by jealously protected borders. During the same period of time the ideas of the Age of Enlightenment spread over the continent. Universalism, humanism, and progress inspired in some countries fierce opposition on the part of social, political, and religious conservatisms, taking firm stand on intransigent positions.

On the eve of the twenty-first century, the world has changed. It seems to lack sense (i.e., intellectual meaning and moral orientation). The partitioning established by the national borders has, to a large extent, made room for new regional entities and for an economic global and worldwide system that too often generates inequality and not a universalism that respects the human being and its environment.

Doubt and even suspicion have replaced the hope of a better future. The tyranny of an omnipresent "here and now" deprives us of the mental distance required to know the past and consider the future. The reassessment of clericalisms, integrisms, and fanaticisms carries with it misunderstanding and violence.

Do we have as Freemasons to forego the attainments and the space of our forebears, the battles of today, and the hopes of tomorrow? It would be a serious error. Thus, it appeared appropriated to the jurisdictions, signatories of the present declaration, to elaborate a founding text, witness of a new era and a reference for future joint action.

Declaration

1. The jurisdictions of the higher Scottish degrees, meeting May 8, 2005, at the Zenith of Geneva, reaffirm solemnly and vigorously their adhesion to the fundamental principles of the Order. They deliberated about their contemporary task, about their specificity and the way and frame in which they work on progression through initiation. Two centuries after the founding of the rite in the tradition of universal Freemasonry, they stress the respect of human dignity, the acceptance in their structure of all Masons of recognized integrity. They exclude discrimination as well as any prejudice or distinction of an ethnical, political, philosophical, or religious nature.

2. Their tradition is based on a Masonic method that is based on a symbolism that is taught and experienced, not imposed but suggested. This symbolism constitutes the common language that enables a joint reflection on human improvement. This reflection overcomes dividing walls, ideological barriers, and doctrinal assumptions and opens a perspective of unlimited research.

3. The Ancient and Accepted Scottish Rite is the most used rite worldwide. It is an initiatory, traditional, and universal Masonic teaching of thirty higher degrees. Its founding principles are fraternity, justice, and the spirit of chivalry.

4. The rite is ruled by sovereign and independent jurisdictions that govern the degrees beyond the initiatory symbolic one of master Mason.

5. The rite adds to its international size the universal value of its principles based on a humanism focusing on the human being, its spiritual thinking and its action. Practicing the rite helps as well to establish links among different cultures and civilizations.

6. The rite, opposing any dogma or any constraining ideology, asserts the need of freedom of conscience as the basic requirement to develop a free spirituality accessed by ongoing research for truth.

7. The rite relies on its principle of progressive improvement of the Mason, on the quest of knowledge of oneself by the initiatory method, added to the willingness to work constantly for the happiness of mankind and its intellectual and moral emancipation.

[Following the above text are the signatures of the representatives of the twenty jurisdictions present in Geneva for the Eighteenth International Conference of the Scottish Rite.]

Appendix VI

Declaration of Basel (June 10, 2012)

On behalf of the Grand Lodge of Austria, the Regular Grand Lodge of Belgium, the Vereinigte Grosslogen von Deutschland, the Grand Lodge of Luxemburg, and the Grand Lodge Alpina of Switzerland, their respective Grand Masters, convened today in Basel, solemnly declare:

1. Following their London declaration of 17 December 2011, the five Grand Lodges have taken the necessary procedural steps for a withdrawal of GLNF's recognition, each Grand Lodge according to its general regulations, by-laws, and constitution. The Grand Lodges regret to have to make this withdrawal official and effective as of today.

2. Under the circumstances, they feel obliged to officially declare that their decision is based on the fact that under its present governance the GLNF has irretrievably slipped its moorings. In actual fact, GLNF's ongoing crisis demonstrates an unforgivable neglect of Masonic principles and Landmarks while the composition of its electoral colleges and the voting procedure have definitely deprived its leadership of all legitimacy, Masonic or otherwise. The recent split-up in its very midst, far from solving GLNF's problems, does only underline its state of decomposition.

   It is with deep sadness that the five Grand Lodges have to acknowledge the demolition of an almost one-hundred-year-old Masonic heritage along with the courageous work of entire generations, and this by the fault of the present leaders of the GLNF for which history will hold them.

3. The five Grand Lodges affirm their conviction that in view of its great Masonic tradition France needs to retrieve its proper place in the universal chain of brotherhood through a bold reconstruction of its Masonic landscape avoiding all further fragmentation.

4. Among all the potential actors of this reconstruction process, the Grande Loge de France could play a major role, having already been greatly esteemed for some time by the five Grand Lodges not only because of the quality of its brethren and their ritual work but also for their vivid and well-known desire to become part of the universal chain of recognized freemasonry.

The five Grand Lodges believe therefore, that there is an historic chance for the Grand Loge de France to realize its aspiration assuming all the necessary choices involved are complied with, especially the need

- to continue to work in accordance with the fundamental principles of regular freemasonry;
- to sever unambiguously remaining links with irregular Obediences;
- to respect the international customs and traditions governing the relation between a Grand Lodge and a Supreme Council.

The five Grand Lodges seriously wish to support and to counsel the Grand Loge de France in this matter and declare their willingness to start negotiations with a view to its eventual recognition.

5. Notwithstanding this declaration, the five Grand Lodges reconfirm their determination not to abandon the very large number of present and former Brethren of the GLNF who wish to practice their traditional Masonry within an administrative framework safely embedded in internationally recognized Freemasonry. Their aspiration as well as the interest of all other brethren willing to become part of a reconstructed regular French Freemasonry shall at all times be near to the heart of the five Grand Lodges and their negotiating representatives.

Appendix VII

Declaration of Vienna (January 29, 2014)

TO THE GRAND LODGES IN FRIENDSHIP

The five grand lodges met in Vienna on these days of January 28 and 29, 2014.

They would first like to remind the French and international Masonic communities that their Declaration of Basel calling for the reconstruction of the Masonic landscape unambiguously asserted the necessary respect for the *"rules and basic principles of the craft"* on the one hand, and openness to *all* Masons seeking to enroll in a sincere, regular Masonic approach.

They observe that today, nearly one-and-one-half years after Basel, both the GNLF and the Confédération Maçonnique de France are committed to their respective paths and have thereby achieved a certain number of major realizations.

These realizations inspire among the brethren concerned an undeniable enthusiasm, thereby demonstrating the necessity to "gather what has been scattered."

Also under consideration today, with respect to numerous contacts with all the parties involved:

That it is necessary to take into account the deep scars that the crisis caused among the brothers whether they are current members of the GLNF, the GLAMF, and the GLIF; the five grand lodges consider these last two as regular because of their origin.

That all parties of the Confédération Maçonnique de France should now determine the suitability of each one, unambiguously confirming both the vocation and purpose of their confederal institution; to wit: international recognition, and on the other hand, their commitment to respect and encourage respect of the rules of Freemasonry permitting this recognition.

That in regard to the remarks of the grand master of the GLNF at various international meetings, his obedience should conscientiously determine his moral responsibility in the face of the consequences of the crisis and work toward the reunification of the regular Masons.

Following this, the grand lodges call on all the parties mentioned above to clarify their position and—taking into account international customs permitting both a confederal model and "the sharing of territory" by a mutual recognition—to unify all the regular Masons in as short a time as possible.

The five grand lodges again affirm their concern about noninterference but also their wishes to establish ties of recognition with those who hold in their hearts the desire to take their responsibility for the good of their brethren and for the good of universal Freemasonry.

Vienna, January 29, 2014.

Grand Lodge of Austria A.F. & A.M., M.W. Bro. Nikolaus Schwarzler, Grand Master

Regular Grand Lodge of Belgium, M.W. Bro. Eli Peeters, Grand Master

United Grand Lodge of Germany, M.W. Bro. Rüdiger Templin, Grand Master

Grand Lodge of Luxembourg, M.W. Bro. Jacques Hansen, Grand Master

Grand Lodge Alpina of Switzerland, M.W. Bro. Jean-Michel Mascherpa, Grand Master

Jean-Michel MASCHERPA
Grand Master

Jacques HANSEN
Grand Master

Eli PEETERS
Grand Master

Ruediger TEMPLIN
Grand Master

Nikolaus SCHWÄRZLER
Grand Master

Appendix VIII

Extracts from the Report of the Commission on Information for Recognition of the American Grand Lodges at the Conference of Baltimore in 2014

Excerpt from the Report of the Commission on Information for Recognition

February 18, 2014

To the Conference of Grand Masters of Masons of North America:

Most Worshipful Brother Chairman:

Most Worshipful and Right Worshipful Brethren:

It is my honor as Chairman of the Commission to present the 60th annual report of the Commission on Information for Recognition. I am pleased to present the other members of this Commission in the order of length of service.

France

It appears that the administrative problems with the Grand Lodge National de Françoise (GLNF) have been resolved. Other constitutional changes will be voted on in April of 2014. In the 2012 report of the Commission, it stated that a "reasonable course of action to consider is to suspend fraternal relations with the GLNF." Based on the resolution of the administrative problems, member Grand Lodges may desire to reconsider that suspension.

Appendix IX

*Letter of the Sovereign Grand Commander Alain de Keghel
to the Northern Jurisdiction*

*Supreme Council; Grand Council
of the Ancient and
Accepted Scottish Rite G∴O∴D∴F∴.*

The Sovereign Grand Commander

Paris, October 18, 2004

To Ill∴ Sov∴ Grand Commander
Walter E. Webber, 33°
Supreme Council, 33°
Ancient Accepted Scottish Rite
Northern Masonic Jurisdiction
P.O. Box 519
LEXINGTON, MA 02420-0519 U.S.A.

Dear Sovereign Grand Commander and Ill∴ Bro∴ Webber,

I take today the initiative to contact you because of very serious concerns fueled by recent news reporting that your Scottish Rite Jurisdiction should have dropped the Degree of Grand Elect Knight Kadosh.

This report has raised consternation and concerns in our Supreme Council. Acting as the direct legitimate Heir of the French Grand Council that issued to Stephen Morin the famous and founding Patent, I wish to urge you to kindly reconsider this decision. The change to the Scottish Rite system of degrees you may have decided, if confirmed, would be a dramatic drop never before experienced worldwide. It would deeply hurt the specific Tradition of our Rite since this Degree is well known as the "ne plus ultra" and has a very specific and rich Masonic meaning.

Since our Supreme Councils have no agreement of reciprocal recognition,

I do not expect any formal answer from you, but I would gladly share with Thousands of Scottish Rite Masons worldwide the joy of reconsideration of this major issue.

With most fraternal greetings I remain

Yours Sincerely

ALAIN DE KEGHEL 33°

SOVEREIGN GRAND COMMANDER

SUPRÊME CONSEIL, GRAND COLLÈGE DU R∴E∴A∴A∴

– G∴O∴D∴F∴

Suprême Conseil, Grand Collège du Rite Écossais
Ancien Accepté – G∴O∴D∴F∴
16 rue Cadet F-75422 PARIS CEDEX 09 – B.P. n° 115 FRANCE
E-mail : amhg@free.fr

Appendix X

Thirty-fifth Anniversary of the George Washington Union

Solemn Statement of Honorary Grand Master Bro∴ Alain de Keghel on the Occasion of the Thirty-fifth Anniversary of George Washington Union Grand Lodge Or∴ Washington, D.C., November 12, 2011

WGM, dear Bro Didier,
Dear SS and BBrr of GWU and of visiting lodges,
Dignitaries in the East,

It was here in the Orient of Washington, D.C., in the year 1996 that we had a dream. A dream inspired from old times and from some old timers. And of course a dream coming from our own souls and inherited from our roots in Masonic tradition and education. But you may wonder why I am referring to 1996 while we today are commemorating the thirty-fifth anniversary of our Masonic body. And you are right. You are right because on December 10, 1976, a small group of American Masons took the first decisive steps in founding in the Or∴ of New York City, a lodge named George Washington Lodge n° 1, dedicated to the spirit of absolute freedom of conscience and of progress. Seemingly, it was in their minds to provide their brethren and sisters a chance to build a new Masonic bridge to overcome some prejudices that were still a kind of limitation of their fundamental creed, which I could here stress again: absolute freedom of conscience. Three brethren, all of them very much dedicated to our philosophy, had the privilege to take this joint initiative, and we have today a sacred obligation to remember their memories because they deserve our eternal recognition for having taken such a founding and fundamental initiative. We have also to remember that the Grand Orient de France supported this initiative in granting the patent in accordance with the agreement signed by Grand Master Serge Behar on August 16, 1977. The General Assembly of the GODF ratified this agreement in September 1978. Because of my age and maybe also of some continued Masonic commitment during the last fifty years, I belong to those who had the privilege to know all of them personally, and it was very inspiring for me and for the transmission of a spirit we all here have inherited. I suggest today that we remember them with brotherly love and that we dedicate our commemoration to their memories. But as we know nobody, no single one, is perfect. The brethren I am referring to today are Alfred Kagan, Harry Hendler, and Raoul Zetler. They all three were members of W∴L∴ L'Atlantide, Or∴ of New York City, the first Masonic lodge belonging to the French Grand Orient de France established in the United States. But additionally, all of them as well belonged to the co-Masonic order DH-AF. For some reasons, more specifically among them the legitimate wish to conduct works in English, but also to include sisters into their tyled communications, they decided to go another way, and doing so they also were shifting from the "male only" tradition of GODF and of W∴L∴ L'Atlantide, allowing in this way sisters not only to share their works but also to be initiated or affiliated with their new lodge. Thus, they decided to take these steps to go another way, and doing so they claimed to act in "the American way." I am not sure that American Masons claiming to keep regular should have agreed—and still today would agree—but it is another question. . . . It was their choice. And in my view it was a big step forward.

Right from the start they were facing the usual problems one encounters when taking a new—and then considered as "revolutionary" or at least radical—initiative. But anyway, they started their work with a lot of idealism, believing in the force of their choice: English should be the only language used during stated communications as in other occasions. The ritual used by them should be that of Droit Humain–American Federation. They were first hosted in the temple of the Gran Logia de Lengua Espanola de los E∴U∴ in New York City. A choice eased by the fact that this Spanish-language lodge of exiled Cuban Masons was from the start a founding member of CLIPSAS. So far so good. But unfortunately, this sympathetic adventure did not last much more than two years of Masonic activities, which were then discontinued. The reasons for that included the lack of support—and it sounds like an understatement—from Masons from the GODF at W∴L∴ L'Atlantide. But, as well, the small group of founding members was failing to attract a mixed American membership from the American civil society and facing the hostile posture of DH-AF. The more, the very conservative G∴L∴ of New York, not having forgotten previous exogenous experiences, like the famous one of French brother Cerneau in the nineteenth century, showed fierce opposition, considering female initiations a "sin" of major irregularity in the spirit of Anderson's Constitutions of 1723. And as a matter of fact, American Masons, likewise the British, still simply do not recognize today the initiation of women, even though some more open-minded British Masons recently stated in Edinburgh, Scotland (May 2007), in a kind of move, admitted that "the Female Masonry as practiced especially in France GLFF could be considered as regular . . . if not practiced by women." In others words, typical British humor mixed with some pragmatism and, maybe, an announcement of a possible move in the next future, when in 2017 Freemasonry will celebrate its tercentennial. Let us wait and see! But we have also to know that mixed co-Masonry as practiced by the GWU and DH-AF still is considered by the UGLE and its followers as the absolute devil. So it is not surprising also for that reason that the DH-AF never succeeded in reaching a real significant membership. This sounds like a paradox in a country like the United States, where the rights of women are often claimed. But it is a matter of fact that American Freemasonry remains very conservative, and not only in this regard. The George Washington Union is at least in this regard an American exception we can altogether proudly claim today. To be perfectly honest, this environment, but additionally some more specific personal reasons as well, which it is not useful today to speculate on, explains why the W∴L∴ George Washington n° 1 very soon went into a long-lasting deep sleep. The lack of support of W∴L∴ L'Atlantide, at this time hostile to any kind of mixed Masonry, for sure did not help, but was not decisive. However, one should not underestimate the capabilities of the three founding members named ahead to be very efficient networkers in France. Their personal fame in the GODF, where the lack of knowledge of America added to the eternal romantic Franco-American dream, allowed them to present themselves as an "American Masonic body" and to join in this capacity with the international federation of CLIPSAS as soon as 1979, and for this reason to keep, year after year, being invited to the closing ceremony of the General Assembly of the GODF in Paris. . . . Which explains that although the George Washington Lodge n° 1 was no longer active, it had a continued, ongoing virtual existence. While being sarcastic, I confess that we, anyway, today benefit from that, for the best, and I strongly support the Treaty of Amity and the membership within CLIPSAS, which belong to our history and are part of our international legitimate recognition as part of the American Masonic landscape, even though we have to be realistic because of our specificity, which makes of us a rather modest planet in the Masonic universe. Some recent proposals we received from the top level from the GLFF confirm that this analysis is not simply wishful thinking and could very soon let us benefit from dual membership for our sisters with the oldest European feminine grand lodge.

But since we are commemorating the thirty-fifth anniversary of the GWU, let us turn back to our history. Said circumstances had as a consequence that despite desperate efforts to assert that George Washington Lodge n° 1 had survived and that, moreover, in 1993 another lodge, Keystone n° 2, was created in the Orient of Colorado Springs, Colorado, and other triangles created in "dream Orients," it, nevertheless, at the end appeared evident that these outings were purely speculative, and it is an understatement to confess today that nothing was really proved of any such Masonic activities. But again, we have today to consider the positive side of this fiction and to remember how a brainstorming session initiated in June 1996 during the Journées d'Amérique du Nord et du Pacifique of the GODF at Los Angeles concluded with the wish to find ways to attract American citizens to our Masonic stream and to get support from them to act according to the principles of CLIPSAS. Or let us say the "adogmatic" way, a neologism, or new wording, forged in the nine ties to prevent any kind of misunderstanding in referring to "liberal Freemasonry," which often sounds leftist in American ears. My personal links with the then grand master of the GODF and the proposals of Deputy Grand Master Raymond Bagnis to get some experienced Masons involved in reactivating George Washington Lodge n° 1 and to make out of it a real George Washington Union reuniting the "different lodges of named union" in order to start a new dynamic, emerged in Washington, D.C., with the enthusiastic support of the two survivors of George Washington Lodge n° 1, Brethren Harry Hendler and Raoul Zetler. I was at this time myself W∴M∴ of La Fayette 89 Lodge of the GODF at Washington, D.C., and recently assigned as a French diplomat at the French permanent mission to the Organization of American States. I had been some ten years earlier a junior member of the Conseil de l'Ordre of the GODF with Grand Master Roger Leray. So I benefited from strong support from GODF leadership, whose policy was to fully endorse the recommendations of the Los Angeles regional meeting of June 1996. So I was kindly and most fraternally invited to take the leadership and all useful steps to reactivate the GWU and to make this work as soon as possible. The Conseil de l'Ordre, or let us say the board of directors of the GODF, provided a special decree for that. It was voted on November 1996 at the seat of the GODF on rue Cadet. I must confess, to be perfectly honest, that I had my doubts about this enterprise precisely because of my knowledge of the international Masonic landscape. But as a brave Mason fully dedicated to our idealistic philosophy, I agreed anyway to commit myself and started involving those few Masons ready to engage with me in this uncertain adventure. One of my first concerns was to get active support from Masons who already had managing experience in American lodges. A working team was soon starting its work to create first a new lodge at the Orient of Washington, D.C. We decided to choose a distinctive name, Liberty 3, as a kind of follow-up of George Washington Lodge n° 1 and Alfred Kagan Lodge n° 2—and of course to elect an American Mason as our first W∴M∴.

Brother Michael Niddam had been a master in an American lodge and agreed. Things were then rapidly developing a new dynamic. We worked hard and very intensively on a new specifically American ritual, first for entered apprentices, because we felt the need to get rid of the DH ritual previously used by W∴L∴ George Washington Lodge n° 1. And instead of questioning the fiction of a "GWU made of several lodges and triangles," we agreed to "continue." This pragmatism made possible a shortcut in conveying a general assembly that would have to vote on reactivating the George Washington

Union and elect a grand master as well as grand officers. The first general assembly took place in October 1996 at my private residence after intense preparation. Brother Harry Hendler was then still claiming to be the active grand master of said obedience, and I was the same day myself elected deputy grand master "ad vitam." But I confess today that I never liked much this "ad vitam," knowing best how short life is and preferring efficiency over the titles many Masons seem to have a great capacity to develop all around the world, and it is not only the privilege of the ever-so-funny American Shriners. . . . The only way to keep in accordance with our Masonic idealism is to work the way we were taught while entering into our Order as entered apprentices: work on ourselves to take part in the development of progress of the society and always look forward. We must today express our thanks to all those Masons whose support and involvement were decisive for the success, so far, of this incredible utopia we have experienced and are celebrating today. I would not be able to mention everyone, but allow me to refer to Brethren Victor Obadia and Pierre Maurice, both past masters of W∴L∴ La Fayette 89, who declined to listen to those who did not accept this new trend disturbing them in their comfortable conservatism and conformism. The force of Masonic conviction was at the end the best guarantee for a constructive and fraternal coexistence based on tolerance and on an agreement voted in W∴L∴ La Fayette 89 after some debates, which belong to history today. The way was then paved for a future I never expected to experience. We soon opened a lodge at the Orient of Los Angeles, we had a very dynamic triangle at the Orient of Chicago under the chairmanship of Brother Jean-Louis Petit, very soon after also a new lodge in San Francisco and another one in Canada. Those having shared with me the unique experience of the initiation of our S∴ Nicolinni will never forget it—for sure she will not. Nor shall we forget the fraternal hospitality of Brother Jean-Louis Petit, who would soon become one of our grand masters, continuing the improvement of the GWU. I will not be able, either, to mention today the names of all the Masons who, having invested a lot of fraternity, of time, of energy, and of idealism, make it possible for the GWU to be what it is today: an independent American Masonic body enjoying full sovereignty and international recognition, mainly because of the quality of the work all dedicated sisters and brethren are performing day after day, restless in our lodges since 1996. You have altogether demonstrated that with hope, faith, and charity almost everything remains possible. I have here to pay also a tribute to Jean-Claude Zambelli, past grand master, and to congratulate you, dear Brother Grand Master Didier Minecci, for the beautiful job you do as our grand master today, along with a good team. And because of my special historical ties with W∴L∴ Liberty 3, let me at least recognize specially our dear Sister Stéphanie Bagot, W∴M∴.

Finally, I have to thank all of you for having invited me today for this commemoration to share with you the fraternal joys of remembering the way we all have been going for the last thirty-five years. I do hope I have not offended anyone with my straight statements. But I believe it is our destiny to look at the world as it is with the eternal hope to make ourselves and our society better. As American Masons used to say, "Let us pray for that."

Good luck to the GWU and let us together continue working hard and fraternally for a better future!

I have spoken.

ALAIN DE KEGHEL

Appendix XI

George Washington Union:
A Progressive American Obedience

History

It was in 1976 (December 10, 1976) that the FF∴ French and American members of the R∴L∴ L'Atlantide of the Orient of New York, who later would join some FF∴-sympathizing Americans, would take the initiative, under the leadership and impetus of the FF∴ Harry Hendler and Alfred Kagan to create an American progressive lodge in New York. This lodge, in the spirit of its initiators, would form the embryo of a future American liberal obedience working in accordance with the precepts of absolute freedom of conscience. This was twenty years ago!

This lodge with the distinctive title of George Washington no. 1 received its exclusive patent from the G∴O∴D∴F∴ in the terms of a convention signed on August 16, 1977, and ratified by the Congress of the Grand Orient in September 1978.

Since 1979, this lodge has been a member of CLIPSAS so as to assert very clearly its liberal Masonic tendencies in both the United States and abroad.

The beginnings of the lodge enjoyed an encouraging activity. Meetings in English took place at a regular monthly pace, following the French rite, and benefited from the diligence of the FF∴ of the R∴L∴ L'Atlantide and of George Washington no. 1, the two lodges working together in total osmosis and in alternation until the end of the 1970s. At that time, or so it seems, following the change of the venerable master of the respectable lodge L'Atlantide, the necessity or rather the wish of the members, perhaps regrettable because it was premature, appeared to disassociate the work of the two lodges. The sudden lack of the relations and support of the R∴L∴ L'Atlantide, essential during the building period of the young American lodge, seems to have caused a big slowdown in this undertaking before all activity over the minimum ceased, so that practically speaking the lodge maintained only its virtual life, to preserve its fragile gains.

The ups and downs, due to the mobility of the FF∴, both French and American, also greatly contributed during this preliminary phase to the weakening of the dynamics of this voluntaristic approach. But these setbacks nonetheless did not prevail over an undertaking that was, by definition, quite difficult on American soil, which was fundamentally hostile to the G∴O∴D∴F∴ (not only but particularly because of the establishment of the R∴L∴ L'Atlantide in New York in violation of the "sacrosanct" rule of territorial exclusivity) and the notion of absolute freedom of conscience, and this American resistance was entirely foreign to the very French value of secularism. However, the lodge has prospered, albeit modestly, over the years. The Keystone no. 2 Lodge was created as an offshoot of the first in 1993, in Colorado Springs, Colorado, followed by the Triangle Alfred Kagen in 1995.

Notes

Preface.
Interpreting American Freemasonry throughout Time

1. Andreas Önnerfors, in Hivert-Messeca, *L'Europe sous l'acacia,* 751–58.

Chapter 1. Freemasonry in Pioneer America

1. Fontanelle, *Discours sur la nature de l'églogue,* 364.
2. Roger, *Cahiers de l'Association Internationale des Etudes Françaises,* 168.

Chapter 2.
At the Order's Origins:
The United Grand Lodge of England

1. Le Moal and Lerbet, *La Franc-maçonnerie,* 26.
2. Lussy, "History of the Supreme Council 33°."
3. Thual, "La complexité du fait Maçonnique."
4. Andreas Önnerfors, in the afterword of Hivert-Messica, *L'Europe sous l'acacia,* vol. II.
5. Mollier, *Note d'analyse interne inedited.*
6. Lepage, *L'Ordre et les obédiences.*
7. Koch, "La Lumière," in *L'Express.*

Chapter 3.
The American Spiritual Infusion and Freemasonry

1. Preuss, *Étude sur la Franc-maçonnerie américaine,* 72–73.

2. Ibid., 324.

3. Hoyos and Morris, *Is It True?*

4. James, *Will to Believe.*

5. Mackey, *Encyclopedia of Freemasonry,* 119.

6. Mackey, *Symbolism of Freemasonry.*

7. Cook, "Review of Factors," 76–78, 81.

Chapter 5.
Black American Freemasonry

1. Tocqueville, *Democracy in America.*

2. Révauger, *Black Freemasonry.*

Chapter 9.
French Freemasonry in North America, Yesterday and Today

1. Brengues, "Les Franc-maçons français."

Bibliography

American Federation of Human Rights. *A History of the American Federation of Human Rights: The Earliest Years with Louis Goaziou.* American Federation of Human Rights/Larkspur Historical Society, Larkspur, Colo.: 1932.

Bernheim, Alain. "Le bicentenaire des Grandes Constitutions de 1786: Essai sur les cinq textes de référence historiques du REAA." *Renaissance traditionnelle,* nos. 69–70 (1987).

———. "Présentation des problèmes historiques du REAA." *Renaissance traditionnelle,* no. 61 (1985).

Bessel, Paul M. "Masonic Recognition Issues." www.bessel.org (accessed February 26, 2017).

Brengues, Jacques. "Les francs-maçons français et les États-Unis d'Amérique à la fin du XVIIIᵉ siècle." *Annales de Bretagne et des pays de l'Ouest* LXXXIV (1977).

Bullock, Steven C. *Revolutionary Brotherhood: Freemasonry and the Transformation of the American Social Order (1730–1840).* Chapel Hill: The University of North Carolina Press, 1998.

Collectif. *Deux siècles de Rite Écossais Ancien et Accepté en France.* Preface by Alain de Keghel. Paris: Éditions Dervy, 2012.

Combes, André. *Histoire de la Franc-maçonnerie au XIXᵉ siècle.* Monaco: Éditions du Rocher, 1998.

Cook, Glen A. "A Review of Factors Leading to Tension between the Church of Jesus Christ of the Latter-Day Saints and Freemasonry." *Philalethes* XLVII, no. 4 (August 1995): 76–78, 81.

Dieterle, E. "Précis historique de 'La Sincérité no. 373.'" Orient of New York (1805–1955).

Doré, André. "Le concordat maçonnique de 1804 ou introduction en France du REAA." *Bulletin du GCDR,* no. 100 (1983).

Le Droit Humain Fédération Canadienne. www.droithumaincanada.org (accessed April 14, 2017).

Fontanelle, Bernard Le Bouvier de. *Discours sur la nature de l'églogue* [Discourse on the Nature of the Pastoral Poem]. Vol. 36. Edited by Bastien.

Graham, John H. *Outlines of the History of Freemasonry in the Province of Quebec.* Whitefish, Mont.: Kessinger Publishing, 2010.

Grand Orient du Québec. "Le Grand Orient du Québec vous souhaite la bienvenue." www.godq.org (accessed February 26, 2017).

Hahn, Conrad. *A Short History of the Conference of Grand Masters of Masons in North America.* Burtonsville, Md.: Masonic Service Association, 1963.

Harris, Ray Baker, 33°. *History of the Supreme Council 33° (Mother Council of the World), Ancient and Accepted Scottish Rite of Freemasonry, Southern Jurisdiction, USA* (1801–1861), Washington, D.C.: Supreme Council 33°, 1964.

Headings, Mildred. *La Franc-maçonnerie française sous la IIIe République.* Monaco: Éditions du Rocher, 1998.

Heaton, Ronald E. *Masonic Membership of the Signers of the Declaration of Independence.* Burtonsville, Md.: Masonic Service Association, 1962.

Hivert-Messeca, Yves. *L'Europe sous l'acacia.* Vol. I. L'Univers Maçonnique Collection. Paris: Éditions Dervy, 2013.

———. *L'Europe sous l'acacia.* Vol. II. L'Univers Maçonnique Collection. Paris: Éditions Dervy, 2014.

———. "REAA: D'une genèse agitée à la suprématie mondiale." *La chaîne d'union,* nos. 14–15 (Automne–Hiver 2001).

Hoyos, Arturo de. *Light on Masonry: The History and Rituals of America's Most Important Masonic Exposé.* Washington, D.C.: Scottish Rite Research Society, 2008.

Hoyos, Arturo de, and S. Brent Morris. *Is it True What They Say about Freemasonry?* Lanham, Md.: M. Evans and Company, 2010.

Isaacson, Walter. *Benjamin Franklin: An American Life.* New York: Simon & Schuster, 2004.

James, William. *The Will to Believe, Human Immortality, and Other Essays in Popular Philosophy.* New York: Dover, 1960.

Kalbach, Robert, and Jean-Luc Gireaud. *L'Hermione: Frigate des Lumières.* Paris: Éditions Dervy, 2004.

Kalbach, Robert. *Les porteurs de lumière: La Fayette, art royal et indépendance américaine.* Paris: Séguier, 2007.

Keghel, Alain de. *La Fayette Franc-maçon.* Paris: AMHG, 2007.

———. "The Time Has Come to Speak. . . . Freemasonry in North America Seen through French Eyes." *The Chain of Union,* special issue (July 2002).

Kellet, P. E., Grand Master. "Internationalism and Freemasonry," *The Builder,* 1915.

Koch, François. "La Lumière." *L'Express.* http://blogs.lexpress.fr/lumiere-franc -macon (accessed February 27, 2017).

Lacorne, Denis. *De la religion en Amérique.* Paris: Gallimard, 2007.

Lassalle, Jean-Pierre. *Célébrations du bicentenaire des Grandes Constitutions de 1786.* Paris: Supreme Conseil pour la France, 1986.

Le Moal, René, and Georges Lerbet. *La Franc-maçonnerie: Une quête philosophique et spirituelle de la connaissance.* Paris: Armand Colin, 2007.

Lepage, Marius. *L'Ordre et les obédiences: Histoire et doctrine de la Franc-maçonnerie.* Paris: Éditions Dervy, 1956.

Ligou, Daniel. *Dictionnaire de la Franc-maçonnerie.* Paris: Presses Universitaires de France, 2006.

Lussy, Florence de. "History of the Supreme Council 33°, Boston, Supreme Council, Northern Masonic Jurisdiction 1938." *Revue de la Bibliothèque Nationale de France,* no. 12 (1984).

Mackey, Albert G. *An Encyclopedia of Freemasonry.* New York–London: The Masonic History Company, 1920.

———. *A Lexicon of Freemasonry.* Washington, D.C.: Walker and James, 1852.

———. *The Symbolism of Freemasonry.* New York: Clark and Maynard, 1882.

Mollier, Pierre. *Note d'analyse interne inedited.* Paris, 2004.

———. "Nouvelles lumières sur la patente Morin." *Renaissance traditionnelle,* nos. 110–11, Paris, 1997.

Morgan, William. *Illustrations of Masonry.* Batavia, N.Y., 1826.

Morris, S. Brent. *Cornerstones of Freedom.* Washington, D.C.: Supreme Council 33°, Southern Jurisdiction, 1993.

———. *The Folger Manuscript: The Cryptanalysis of an American Masonic Manuscript.* Bloomington Ill.: Masonic Book Club, 1993.

———. "Les hauts grades aux États-Unis: 1730–1830, Scottish Rite Research Society, Washington, D.C." *Renaissance traditionnelle,* nos. 110–11 (April–July 1997).

———, ed. *Heredom: The Transactions of the Scottish Rite Research Society.* Vols. I–XX. Washington, D.C.: The Scottish Rite Research Society, 1998–2012.

————. *Masonic Philanthropies: A Tradition of Caring.* Washington, D.C.: The Supreme Councils 33°, Northern Masonic Jurisdiction and Southern Masonic Jurisdiction, 1997.

Muraskin, William Alan. *Middle Class Blacks in a White Society: Prince Hall Freemasonry in America.* Oakland: University of California Press, 1975.

Pietre-Stones Review of Freemasonry. www.freemasons-freemasonry.com (accessed February 26, 2017).

Pike, Albert, 33°. *The Book of Words.* Washington, D.C.: The Scottish Rite Research Society, 1999.

————. *Grand Constitutions of Freemasonry.* Washington, D.C.: Ancient and Accepted Rite, Southern Jurisdiction, 1857.

Preuss, Arthur. *Étude sur la Franc-maçonnerie américaine.* Paris: Bureaux de Revue internationale des sociétés secrètes, 1908.

Prichard, Samuel. *Masonry Dissected.* London, 1730. https://freemasonry.bcy.ca /ritual/prichard.pdf (accessed February 28, 2017).

Révauger, Cécile. *Noirs et Francs-maçons: Comment la ségrégation raciale s'est installée chez les frères américains.* Preface by Margaret C. Jacob. Paris: Éditions Dervy, 2014. L'Univers Maçonnique Collection, supervised by René Le Moal. Translated into English by Jon E. Graham as *Black Freemasonry.* Rochester, Vt.: Inner Traditions, 2016.

Roberts, Allen E. *House Undivided: The Story of Freemasonry and the Civil War.* Richmond, Va.: Macoy, 1961.

Roger, Jacques. *Cahiers de l'Association International des Etudes Françaises.* Vol. XX. Paris: Les Belles Lettres, 1968.

Sadler, Henry. *Faits et fables Maçonniques.* 1887. Reprint, Paris: Editions Vitiano, 1973.

Saint Bris, Gonzague. *La Fayette.* Paris: Gallimard, 2007.

Saunier, Éric. *Encyclopédie la Franc-maçonnerie.* Paris: Le Livre de Poche/Librairie Générale Française, 2000.

Servan-Schreiber, Jean-Jacques. *Le défi américain.* Paris: Denoël, 1968.

Tabbert, Mark A. *American Freemasons: Three Centuries of Building Communities.* New York: New York University Press, 2005.

Thual, François. "La complexité du fait maçonnique." Special issue, "Les francs-maçons, les loges et le monde." *Géopolitique: Revue de l'Institut International de Géopolitique,* no. 97 (2007).

Tocqueville, Alexis de. *Democracy in America.* Indianapolis, Ind.: Hackett, 2000.

Van Buren Voorhis, Harold. *The Story of Scottish Rite of Freemasonry.* New York: Press of Henry Emmerson, 1965.

Van Doren, Carl. *Benjamin Franklin.* New York: The Viking Press, 1938.

Waits, Arthur Edward. *A New Encyclopedia of Freemasonry.* New York: Wings Books, 1996.

Walgren, Kent. "An Historical Sketch of Pre-1851 Louisiana Scottish Rite Masonry." In *Heredom: The Transactions of the Scottish Rite Research Society,* edited by S. Brent Morris. Vol. IV. Washington, D.C.: The Scottish Rite Research Society, 1995.

Walkes, Joseph A., Jr. *Black Square and Compass.* N.p.: Walkes Book Company, 1980.

Watkins, Larissa P. *International Masonic Periodicals (1738–2005): A Bibliography of the Library of the Supreme Council, 33° S.J.* Washington, D.C.: Library of the Supreme Council, 33°, Southern Jurisdiction, 2006.

Webb, Thomas Smith. *The Freemason's Monitor of Illustrations of Masonry.* Salem, Mass.: John Cushing, 1821.

Wesley, Charles H. *Prince Hall: Life and Legacy.* Washington, D.C.: United Supreme Council 33°, South Jurisdiction, Prince Hall Affiliated, 1983.

Zetler, Raoul. Précis historique "L'Atlantide 1900–2000" (unpublished book, New York, 1999).

Index of Names

Numbers in *italics* preceded by *pl.* indicate color insert plate numbers.

Subject Index

Numbers in *italics* preceded by *pl.* indicate color insert plate numbers.